A KEY TO THE DOCTRINE OF
THE EUCHARIST

A KEY
to the
DOCTRINE
of the
EUCHARIST

DOM ANSCAR VONIER, O.S.B.

Angelico Press

For information, address:
Angelico Press, Ltd. • 169 Monitor St. • Brooklyn, NY 11222
www.angelicopress.com

Paperback: 979-8-88677-086-5
Hardback: 979-8-88677-087-2

Cover design by Michæl Schrauzer

IMPRIMATUR

CUM Censor a Nobis deputatus rite recognoverit opus
cui titulus *A Key to the Doctrine of the Eucharist*, lingua
anglica, A Rm̃o Patre Dño Anschario Vonier, O.S.B.,
Abbate Monasterii Buckfastriensis conscriptum, nihilque
contra fidem et mores in eo reprehenderit, quantum ad
Nos attinet imprimi permittimus.

Datum Ex Asceterio S Specus,
Die 1 *Martii*, 1925.

D. ROMUALDUS SIMO, O.S.B.
Abbas Proc. et Vicarius Generalis.

D. HIERONYMUS HAULER, O.S.B.
Pro Consult.

a Secretis.

NIHIL OBSTAT:
THOMAS MCLAUGHLIN, S.T.D.
Censor deputatus.

IMPRIMATUR:
EDM. CAN. SURMONT
Vicarius generalis.

WESTMONASTERII,
die 5 *Februarii*, 1925.

CONTENTS

CONTENTS

FOREWORD

THE study of the Eucharistic theology may be approached in various ways and from different motives. There is the task of the apologist of Catholic dogma, who sets out to prove from the Scriptures and from tradition the truth of the Church's position in her belief in the Real Presence. Then there are the labours of the speculative theologian, who has set his heart on elucidating the mystery of faith with all the wisdom of a long tradition of Catholic thought. The devotional writer has given us the largest output of Eucharistic literature of all those who have tried to serve the cause of this sublime article of faith.

My own aim in presenting these pages to the Catholic public is neither apologetic nor strictly speculative, nor do I intend to write a book of devotion. It seems to me that there is room for a book which has for its purpose to point out the true setting of the Eucharistic mystery in

the economy of the supernatural life, and this
is the task I have laid upon myself.

The splendid things of our faith, even when
held loyally and devoutly, may be visualised
inaccurately because they are not seen in that
setting in which they came to us from God.
Right visualising of the Eucharistic doctrine is
the one thing I think most necessary in our days,
and to this end I am devoting my humble
labours in what I am about to say.

An intense wish to instruct will be the only
undisputed merit of this book, and so I may be
quite frank from the very outset, and tell my
reader in a few phrases my whole plan.

I want to make it clear that the Eucharistic
doctrine is seen in its true supernatural propor-
tions then only if we study it in the light of the
great sacramental doctrine of the Church.
This, no doubt, will seem a truism, but there is
much more in it than appears at first sight.
It really means a definite kind of visualisation
of the Eucharist, not as common as one might
imagine. I hope to prove to the reader's
satisfaction that the Eucharistic sacrifice itself
is seen in its true light then when sacramental
notions are made use of to express it. And

this means a very consistent and a very distinct way of considering the divine sacrifice of Mass.

I am doing no original work; far from me to have such pretensions; all I hope to do is to reproduce faithfully the mental attitude of the great theological age of which S Thomas Aquinas is the king.

I have taken the liberty of choosing for my title " A Key to the Doctrine of the Eucharist." I do not think that this need sound pretentious; the key is merely the one far-reaching principle which enables S Thomas to open out such vistas into the great mystery of faith. The sacramental principle is truly my key, and I shall be fully repaid if I succeed in making my reader see the Eucharist in that simple light in which the ages of faith saw it. We ought to be able to state the Eucharist in direct, explicit, well-defined language; there ought to be no uncertainties about it. Every Christian ought to have it in his power to express what the Eucharist is and what it is not. To my thinking this can only be obtained if the whole Eucharistic doctrine be stated in terms of sacramental import.

Sacraments are for our daily use and our daily

work; we know when we receive them, and we know what we receive through them. The Eucharistic mystery, great as it is, ought to be likewise within the reach of ordinary thought and speech. This result, of course, only comes at the end of stern thinking. Behind the clear phrases which make it possible for our Catholic people to profess their belief in a way that means so much to them, there is the vast work of adjusting theological concepts, of comparing spiritual things with spiritual things, and of finding the centre of a wonderful network of living thought.

It may seem almost ironical to write a book of intense thought, as the following pages must of necessity be, with a view to produce a simple, workable expression of the Eucharistic doctrine; but is not this the law of all clear and living truth ? does not the thing that has become an article of ordinary use presuppose painful and immense pioneer work ? Our Catholic doctrines can afford to be simple because the greatest minds have conspired in the effort of bringing them down from heaven to the level of our daily life.

If it is my duty to teach a Catholic child his

Catechism, I will tell him that at Mass there is offered up to God the Body and the Blood of Jesus Christ as a sacrifice. This is a lesson the child will understand at once; he knows that the Body and Blood of Christ were separated at one time, as the story of the Cross is easily grasped by the Catholic child; he soon learns something about the sacrifices of the Old Law; so this proposition that the Body and Blood of Christ are offered up as sacrifice is by no means beyond the measure of his little mind. Left in this elemental form the theological proposition may follow a man through his whole life, and he will never be puzzled by it, just as he is not confused by that other thing he has learned in childhood, that his soul had been cleansed by the water of Baptism, or that his sins were forgiven him whenever he went to Confession in sincerity of heart. The statement that the Body and Blood of Christ are offered up in sacrifice to God is a clear, direct issue. The question for us Catholics is whether the thing we love under the name of Mass can be really stated in this elemental fashion without injury to, or diminution of, divine truth. If Mass is all that and only that, the Body and Blood of Christ offered up in sacrifice, then our Catholic worship becomes easy. It has a classical simplicity and primitiveness; there is no element in it that can bewilder our thoughts or confuse the issues. A whole nation may hold that the Body of Christ and the Blood of Christ are offered up with a definite rite, well known to everybody. There could be no two ways of understanding an idea presented with such extreme literalness, because every man would know what is meant by Christ's Body, what is understood by Christ's Blood, what is signified by a sacrifice.

When Christ announced in the synagogue of Capharnaum that he would give his Flesh to eat and his Blood to drink, there was no doubting his meaning. His hearers understood him: they murmured: they called it a hard saying, and many of them no longer walked with him. Men can always behave in such a fashion; my concern is not with them in that mood. I have a more agreeable mission to fulfil; I want to prove to the believer that after everything has been said, after a careful study of all the issues and of all the implications of so great a mystery as is the Eucharist, we have all of us to come back to our spiritual infancy; we have to hold that fulness of Eucharistic truth is contained in this, that Christ's Body and Christ's Blood, nothing more, nothing less, nothing holier, nothing lower, is offered up on the Catholic Altar. The Catholic sacrificial rite is what all sacrificial rites have always been, a separation of the living blood from the living body; the superior privilege of Christendom is in the infinite sanctity of the two things, Body and Blood. This will be our conclusion, and I am sure my reader will thank me for telling him from the very start that he will come back to the point of departure.

ANSCAR VONIER, O.S.B.,
Abbot.

BUCKFAST ABBEY.
Easter, 1925.

A KEY TO THE DOCTRINE OF THE EUCHARIST

CHAPTER I

FAITH

THE Catholic doctrine of the Eucharist is a particular instance of the more universal problem of the mode of our union with Christ. We take for granted the Incarnation and the Atonement on the Cross; we take for granted, too, that the Son of God through his death has redeemed mankind in general and has satisfied for sin; we know that in Christ there is plentiful redemption; such things are for us unchallengeable and universal articles of belief which may be called God's side of the problem, that aspect of truth which is turned heavenward. The universal truths thus enunciated leave untouched that other problem of our own individual share in the treasures of redemption—how do individual men come into contact with that great Christ who is redemption personified? There is evidently in the Christian doctrine of redemption an element so absolute that it stands by itself, quite independent of man's benefit in it. Before it is at all possible to think of man's enrichment through the grace of Christ's redemption we have to assume that much greater result of Christ's sacrifice on the Cross which is aptly stated in the term "atonement," by which is meant, not directly the benefit of man, but the benefit of God: that full restoration of the thing lost to God through man's sin, his honour and glory. Christ's act on the Cross has given back to God all that was ever taken away from God by man, and the divine rights have been fully restored.

It is not an absurd hypothesis to think of Christ's great act of atonement as having an exclusively divine side—that is to say, Christ could have died on the Cross with the exclusive purpose of giving back to the Father all the glory which the Father had lost through man's transgression, without the human race being in any way the better for it. But this is merely an hypothesis, though a perfectly rational one. Catholic doctrine says that Christ's sacrifice, besides being an atonement, was also a salvation, —in other words, a buying back into spiritual liberty of the human race which had become the slave of Evil. But even this aspect of

Christ's divine act, though a perfectly human aspect, is still a universal aspect; salvation is primarily for mankind as a species; the entry of the individual into the redemptive plan remains still to be effected. How am I to be linked up effectively with that great mystery of Christ's death? When shall I know that Christ is not only Redeemer, but also my Redeemer? Mere membership with the human race does not link me up with Christ, though it be true that Christ died for the whole race. This membership is indeed a remote condition—*sine qua non* —of my becoming one day a member of Christ, but a member of Christ I shall not become unless some new realities be brought into play.

The new realities which make the link between me and Christ are, in the words of S Thomas, faith and the sacraments: " The power of Christ's passion is linked up with us through faith and through the sacraments. This, however, in different ways: for the linking up which is by faith takes place through an act of the soul, whilst the linking up which is by the sacraments takes place through the use of external things." This passage is of such paramount importance to the subject that I may be justified in presenting the reader with the Latin text: " Virtus passionis Christi copulatur nobis per fidem, et sacramenta: differenter tamen; nam continuatio, quae est per fidem, fit per actum animae: continuatio autem, quae est per sacramenta, fit per usum exteriorum rerum."*

This is a favourite idea of S Thomas, that faith is truly a contact with Christ, a real, psychological contact which, if once established, may lead man into the innermost glories of Christ's life. Without this contact of faith we are dead unto Christ, the stream of his life passes us by without entering into us, as a rock in the midst of a river remains unaffected in the most turbulent rush of waters.

This contact of faith makes man susceptible to the influences of Christ; under normal conditions it will develop into the broader contact of hope and charity; but it is the first grafting of man on Christ which underlies all other fruitfulness. Till the contact of faith be established the great redemption has not become our redemption; the things of Christ are not ours in any true sense; we are members of the human race, but we are not members of Christ.

This contact of faith is, indeed, the most potent supernatural reality. It does not belong to my subject to enter into a discussion as to the reasons why one man has faith whilst

* *Summa*, III, Q. lxii, Art. vi.

4

another is without faith; nor do I propose to state that minimum of faith which is indispensable in order to establish true contact between the soul and Christ. It is sufficient unto our purpose to know that a man who has faith has laid his hand on the salvation of Christ. It is the most universal way of coming into touch with the redemption of the Cross; it is an approach which is possible from every direction, from the past as well as from the present. Mary, the Mother of God, through her faith, entered into Christ's passion in the very moment of time when it took place; Adam, in his very fall, plunged into it headlong; and it will be present to the last human generation through that wonderful act of the soul of which S Thomas speaks in the above text. Whether we say that Christ will suffer—*passurus est*, or whether we say that Christ has suffered—*passus est*, is quite immaterial to the immediateness of contact by faith. " As the ancient Fathers were saved through faith of the coming Christ, so are we also saved through faith of the Christ who has already been born and has suffered " (" Sicut antiqui Patres salvati sunt per fidem Christi venturi; ita et nos salvamur per fidem Christi jam nati, et passi ").*

* III, Q. lxi, Art. iv.

I feel that we are less habituated in our times to think of faith as a kind of psychic link between the soul and Christ; yet such is the traditional concept of that wonderful gift. Anyone who has faith is in the supernatural state, and therefore is directly in touch with Christ's life, though he be otherwise in a state of mortal sin. The Council of Trent has taken great trouble to make clear this point of Catholic ethics. A man ceases to be Christ's solely through the sin of infidelity; he does not cease to be Christ's through any other sin, however heinous. As long as his faith is a true faith he remains a member of Christ's mystical Body, though there be grievous sores of mortal sins in him. Through that faith, which nothing can kill except the formal sin of infidelity, he keeps so near to the mystery of Christ's death on the Cross that his recovery from the snare of sin, even grievous sin, is a normal process of supernatural life, not a miraculous one. It is true that the faith of the believing Christian in the state of mortal sin is a *fides informis*, a faith devoid of the higher vitalities of charity, yet it is a real faith. Unless we grasp that function of faith as the psychic link between Christ and the soul, Catholicism becomes unintelligible. The Church would become, as it did in Lutheran theology, an adventitious gathering of the elect. The Church is constituted primarily through faith, and her powers are for those who possess that responsiveness of soul called faith. If we believe the Church to possess might enough to wipe away sin, we suppose, *ipso facto*, that sin is compatible with the mystical membership.

Actual incorporation with Christ, according to S Thomas, has a threefold degree; the first is through faith, the second is through the charity of life, the third is through the possession of heaven.*

It is true that the whole tendency of faith is towards charity, that faith without charity cannot save us ultimately; none the less, charity cannot exist in man without faith, whilst there may be true faith in man without actual charity. All this goes to demonstrate that there is in faith an instrumental side, enabling man to open unto himself the door that leads to perfect union with Christ. There is no such instrumental side in charity, as charity is not a means towards the possession of God, but is, on the contrary, actual possession of God. S Thomas calls faith an indispensable endowment of the soul, because it is the beginning or principle of spiritual life: " Fides est necessaria tanquam principium spiritualis vitae."†

* III, Q. viii, Art. iii.   † II, ii, Q. xvi, Art i ad 1.

This peculiar position of faith in the spiritual order as a kind of tool of supreme excellence will be seen in a more complete light when we shall come to ask ourselves the question whether there be another such set of means for man to get at Christ's redemptive life. Once more let it be emphasised that through the possession of charity we do not only get at Christ, but that we are actually in Christ. Charity is not an instrument, whilst faith has an instrumental role.

The sacraments are truly another set of means for that final object, to be united with Christ in charity. The sacraments complete and render more efficacious that instrumentality of faith just spoken of: they do not supersede the instrumentality of faith, but they render such instrumentality more real, if possible, and certainly more infallible in its effect. The relative position of faith and sacraments in bringing about man's justification through charity is an interesting theological question of which we shall have more to say by-and-by. The sacraments are essentially sacraments of the faith, *sacramenta fidei*, as S Thomas invariably calls them; both faith and sacraments have that power of divine instrumentality which will open to man the treasure-house of Christ's redemption.

FAITH

I cannot end this chapter without translating from S Thomas a beautiful passage in which he describes God's action, which he calls grace, keeping faith alive in the soul of even the sinner: " Grace produces faith not only when faith begins to exist in the soul for the first time, but also whilst it abides in the soul permanently . . . God works the justification of man in the way in which the sun produces light in the air. Grace, therefore, when it strikes with its rays the one who is already a faithful believer is not less efficacious than when it comes for the first time to the unbeliever, because in both it is its proper effect to produce faith: in one case strengthening it and giving it increase, in the other case creating it as an entirely new thing."*

The sun of divine grace once above the horizon sends forth the ray of faith into the minds of men, and nothing can resist it except blind obstinacy and infidelity.

* II, ii, Q. iv, Art. iv ad 3m.

CHAPTER II

SACRAMENTS

THERE is an excellent definition of the nature of the sacraments in the sixty-first Question of the third Part of the *Summa* of S Thomas, fourth Article: " Sacraments are certain signs protesting that faith through which man is justified " (" Sunt autem sacramenta quaedam signa protestantia fidem, qua justificatur homo "). Such a definition makes the transition from the role of faith to the role of the sacraments a very natural and easy one. The power of the sacraments could never be dissociated from the power of faith; the two supernatural agencies move forward hand in hand. A sacrament is always an external sign that is a most real witness of that more recondite quality of the soul, the faith that justifies man by bringing him into contact with Christ.

Two questions become paramount here: Firstly, why should there be such external witnessing to or protestation of the faith ? Secondly, to what extent shall we give to those signs literalness in their efficacy of signification ?

The second point as it is settled either in one way or the other makes all the difference between Catholicism and Protestantism, or, it may even be said, between Judaism and Christianity. In one way or another this will be the main burden of this work; but, for the moment, let us dwell on that other aspect of the matter, the radical oneness of the Catholic theory concerning the means of justification. Faith and sacraments are indissolubly united, though faith may be called the vaster, the older, the more universal reality. The sacramental system is grafted on faith; it is essentially the executive of our faith; it is, shall we say, the reward of faith. Because of her faith the Church is granted those further powers of reaching Christ which make Christ not only the object of mental apprehension, but of physical possession; the sacramental thing is granted to those who have faith; such as the sequel of Christ's teaching in the sixth chapter of S John's Gospel. He who does the work of God by believing in him whom the Father has sent is the one to whom Christ will give his Flesh to eat and his Blood to drink. We may apply here that general principle concerning spiritual goodness which Christ enunciates more than once: " To every one that hath shall be given, and he shall abound, but from him that hath not, that also which he seemeth to have shall be taken away."* Because of her abundant faith the Church is given the further riches of her sacraments. At no time are faith and the sacraments dissociated; what might appear at first sight to be the exception to the rule is only a more profound application of it, I mean Baptism bestowed on infants. S Thomas, following S Augustine, falls back on the faith of the Church herself in order to keep intact the union between faith and the sacraments of faith. " In the Church of the Saviour the little ones believe through others, as through others they contract those sins which are washed out in Baptism "; these are words of S Augustine quoted by S Thomas in Question lxviii, Article ix ad 2m, and the medieval Doctor completes the theology of the earlier Father with the following pregnant words: " The faith of the whole Church is of profit to the little one through the operation of the Holy Ghost, who makes the Church into one and makes the one share the goods of the other " (" Fides autem unius, immo totius Ecclesiae, parvulo prodest per operationem Spiritus Sancti, qui unit Ecclesiam, et bona unius alteri communicat") There

* Matt. xxv 29

could hardly be a more incongruous reproach brought against the Catholic Church than the accusation that through her great insistence on the sacramental life she diminishes the power of faith.

It is properly the Puritan, not the Protestant, who is the enemy of the sacramental system taken in the wider aspect of that Thomistic definition with which we opened this chapter. For the Puritan, faith is not in need of any help or any adjuncts. The reasons given by the Catholic theologians for the presence in the Christian dispensation of these external signs of the internal faith are chiefly psychological; they contend that man's nature being what it is, sacraments are indispensable to a full life of faith. S Thomas has a threefold reason for the institution of the sacraments: " Sacramenta sunt necessaria ad humanam salutem, *triplici ratione.*"* But this threefold reason is really one reason, fallen man's psychology: firstly, the condition of man's nature, being a composite of spirit and sense; secondly, man's estate, which is slavedom to material things and which is to be remedied by the spiritual power inside the material thing; thirdly, man's activities, so prone to go astray in external interests, finding

* III, Q. lxi, Art. i.

in the sacraments a true bodily exercise which works out for salvation.

Nothing would be easier than to develop this subject with all the fascination of human psychology coming into play; the sacramental life of the Church is truly a perfect understanding of man's needs. Sacraments are, through their very nature, an extension of the Incarnation, a variant of that mystery expressed in the words: " And the Word was made flesh and dwelt among us." Is not the Son of God made man the Sacrament *par excellence*, the *magnum sacramentum*, the invisible made visible? " And evidently great is the mystery of godliness, which was manifested in the flesh, was justified in the spirit, appeared unto angels, hath been preached unto the Gentiles, is believed in the world, is taken up in glory."*

The definition of the sacrament quoted above, that it is a protestation of the faith which is in us, is not the whole definition of the Christian sacrament, though it may be considered as a complete definition of the sacrament in its widest meaning. S Thomas never hesitates in giving to some of the major rites of the Old Law the name of sacrament, always making it quite clear that the power of these ancient

* 1 Tim. iii 16.

sacraments never went beyond signifying the things of the patriarchal faith, whilst the Christian sacrament has a much higher degree of signification, a signification that has effectiveness associated with it. It would be quite unwise and very ungenerous not to grant to the ancient rites instituted by God sacramental dignity of at least an inferior degree; they all were external signs of the faith in the coming redemption. They were tremendous helps to that faith, though they were not direct causations of grace.

S Thomas divides the life of mankind into four seasons—the state of innocence before the fall, the state of sin before Christ, the state of sin after Christ, and the state of bliss in heaven. No sacraments are necessary in the first and in the last state; sacraments are necessary to man in the two middle states. But it is in the " state of sin after Christ " that sacraments reach their perfection; the seven sacraments of the Christian dispensation are sacraments in the highest sense, because, besides signifying the grace which is the inheritance of faith, they also contain that grace and cause it: " Nostra autem sacramenta gratiam continent, et causant."*

An objector seems to find fault with the

* III, Q. lxi, Art iv ad 2m.

theory that God has given to man different sacraments before Christ and different sacraments after Christ. Does this not argue mutability in the divine will? The answer of S Thomas is quaint, but it is a perfect synthesis of that vaster view of the sacramental system which makes of the sacrament a thing as old as the world: " To the third objection let us answer: that the father of the family is not said to be of changeable disposition because he gives different orders to his household according to the variety of seasons, and does not command the same work to be done in summer and in winter; thus there is not mutability in God's doings because he institutes one set of sacraments after the coming of Christ and another set of sacraments in the time of the Old Law; for these latter were fitting as prefigurements of grace, whilst the former are calculated to show forth grace already present amongst us."*

* III, Q. lxi, Art. iv ad 3m.

CHAPTER III

THE POWER OF SACRAMENTAL SIGNIFICATION

IT is the very essence of a sacrament to be a sign; it is its proper definition. "We speak now specifically of sacraments as far as they imply a relationship of sign " (" Specialiter autem nunc loquimur de sacramentis, secundum quod important habitudinem signi ").* Let us never deprive a sacrament, even the most excellent sacrament, of this constitutional property of relationship of sign. The greatest realist in the Catholic theology of the sacraments, if he be at all orthodox, proclaims boldly his faith, I do not say in the symbolical nature of the sacrament, but in the demonstrative nature of the sacrament as a sign, or, if we like the word better, in the representative nature of the sacrament as a sign. As we shall see by-and-by, this power of signification inside the one and the same sacrament is not simple but multiple, the sacramental element signifying in various ways and also signifying various

* III, Q. lx, Art. i.

things; yet there is a certain definiteness, a clearly outlined circle of signification, which has been traced by the hand of God. It is the divine institution which is responsible directly for the selection of those signs which, again in the words of S Thomas, are given us for a more explicit signification of Christ's grace, through which the human race is sanctified: "Ad expressiorem significationem gratiae Christi, per quam humanum genus sanctificatur."* The angelic Doctor adds, with that true liberality of mind so specially his own, that this clear circumscribing of the sacramental signs does not in any way narrow down the road of salvation, because the things which are of indispensable use in the sacraments are commonly to be had, or may be procured, with very little trouble.† Sacraments, then, are true signs from heaven. In no other sphere of human reality does the external thing become such a messenger of the internal thing. There is in Question lx, Article iii, a passage of S Thomas which may be called truly classical as stating the power of signification proper to the sacraments; its importance justifies me in giving the Latin first, in spite of its length, to be followed by a translation: "Respondeo dicendum, quod, sicut

* III, Q. lx, Art. v ad 3m. † *Ibid.*

dictum est (*art. praec.*,) sacramentum proprie dicitur quod ordinatur ad significandam nostram sanctificationem, in qua *tria* possunt considerari: videlicet ipsa *causa* sanctificationis nostrae, quae est passio Christi; et *forma* nostrae sanctificationis, quae consistit in gratia, et virtutibus; et ultimus *finis* sanctificationis nostrae, qui est vita aeterna. Et haec omnia per sacramenta significantur; unde sacramentum est et signum rememorativum ejus quod praecessit, scilicet passionis Christi, et demonstrativum ejus quod in nobis efficitur per Christi passionem, scilicet gratiae, et prognosticum, idest praenuntiativum futurae gloriae." (" My answer is, as has been already said, that the sacrament, properly so-called, is the thing ordained to the purpose of signifying our sanctification; in this *three* phases may be taken into consideration, namely—the *cause* of our sanctification, which is the passion of Christ; the *essence* of our sanctification, which consists in grace and virtue; and then the ultimate *goal* of our sanctification, which is eternal life. Now these three things are signified by the sacraments; therefore a sacrament is a commemorative sign of what has gone before, I mean the passion of Christ, and a demonstrative sign of what is being brought about in us through the passion of Christ, that is grace, and a prognostic, that is a prophetic sign, of the future glory.")*

Every sacrament, then, announces something; it brings back the past, it is the voice of the present, it reveals the future. If the sacrament did no longer proclaim as a sign something which is not seen, it would not be a sacrament; in every sacrament there is a past, a present, and a future; the death of Christ is its past; supernatural transformation is its present; eternal glory is its future. It can embrace heaven and earth, time and eternity, because it is a sign; were it only a grace it would be no more than the gift of the present hour; but being a sign the whole history of the spiritual world is reflected in it: " For as often as you shall eat this bread and drink the chalice, you shall show the death of the Lord, until he come."† What S Paul says of the Eucharist about its showing forth a past event is true in other ways of every other sacrament. The text we have transcribed from S Thomas is applied by him to every one of the seven sacraments.

Let us make a comparison in order to elucidate more completely this all-important role of the sacraments as being signs of God. If my heart be touched by God's grace, such a spiri-

* III, Q. lx, Art. iii.　　　　† I Cor. xi 26.

tual phenomenon, excellent and wonderful as it may be, is not a sign of anything else; it is essentially a thing of the present, and ends, as it were, in itself. It has no relationship of significance with anything either past, present, or future. Such is not the case with the sacraments; through them it has become possible to condense far distant things in one point; through them historic acts of centuries ago are renewed for us with great reality, and we anticipate the future in a very definite way. All this is possible through the power of the sign, which power, shall we say, becoming most modern, " films " the distant thing, and brings it before us at the present hour.

" O sacrum convivium, in quo Christus sumitur; recolitur memoria passionis ejus: mens impletur gratia, et futurae gloriae nobis pignus datur " (" O sacred Banquet, wherein Christ is received, the memory of his passion is kept, the mind is filled with grace, and there is given unto us a pledge of the coming glory "). This verse from the Office of the Blessed Sacrament, when compared with the above text of the *Summa*, betrays at once its Thomistic origin. But though the Eucharist does that function of cosmic representation in the spiritual order in a more excellent degree, all the other sacraments

21

do it in their several ways. All the sacraments give us the blessed power of stepping outside the present. Much confusion of thought in the doctrine of the sacraments, and particularly in the doctrine of the Eucharist, would be spared us if we never let go of that elemental definition of the sacrament, that it is a relationship of signification. Whatever reality there is in a sacrament is deeply modified by this rule of signification. Baptism, to quote only one sacrament, is not any kind of cleansing of the soul, but it is a cleansing of the soul which is a burial with Christ and which is a resurrection with Christ. Baptism is not only the present, but also the past and the future. " Know you not that all we who are baptised in Christ Jesus are baptised in his death ? For we are buried together with him by baptism into death: that, as Christ is risen from the dead by the glory of the Father, so we also may walk in newness of life. For if we have been planted together in the likeness of his death, we shall be also in the likeness of his resurrection."*

The current definition of the sacrament as an external sign of an internal grace would certainly be too narrow a definition for S Thomas if by internal grace we meant nothing but the

* Rom. vi 3.

actual transformation of the soul. This would only be one-third of the sacramental function. But if by internal grace we also mean the cause of grace—*i.e.*, Christ's passion—and the goal of grace—*i.e.*, eternal life—then the definition may be considered as complete. But to limit the power of significance of the sacrament to the present moment only, to the transformation of the soul at the time when the sacrament is applied to man, would be an unwarranted minimising of the sacramental doctrine, and would make much of the scriptural language unintelligible. How, for instance, could the Eucharist be a memory of Christ if it were merely a supernatural feeding of the soul at the present moment? When Christ said: " Do this for a commemoration of me,"* he gave the Eucharist an historic import which is not to be found in a mere spiritual raising up of the individual soul. A commemoration is essentially a sign, a monument, something related to a definite act or person of the past.

S Thomas lays down as an axiom that a sacrament is always a thing of the senses.† A merely spiritual thing, an act of our intellect or will, could never fulfil that role of sign which is so essential to the sacrament; the sign, on

* Luke xxii 19.   † III, Q. lx, Art. iv.

the contrary, is an external manifestation of the intellectual process of thought and volition: " Effectus autem intelligibiles non habent rationem signi."* In the same passage S Thomas quotes from S Augustine a very succinct definition of what a sign is: " A sign is that which, besides the impression it makes on the senses, puts one in mind of something else." When I see the baptismal water poured on the head of the catechumen, and when I hear the words of the priest who does the christening, if I am a man of faith, my mind, roused by these external rites and signs, travels a long way. I go back to the Jordan, where Christ is being baptised; I go back to Calvary, where blood and water issue from the side of Christ; my mind leaps forward to that people who stand before the Throne of God in white robes which have been washed in the Blood of the Lamb; and, more audacious still, my mind gazes right into the innermost soul of the catechumen and distinguishes that soul from all other non-baptised souls, through that spiritual seal which makes it a member of Christ. The sacramental sign is pregnant with all that spiritual vision of my faith.

When we speak of signs, we mean, of course,

* III, Q. lx, Art. iv ad 1m.

words as well as things; the words are often necessary to complete the signification of the thing. " A repetition of words, when words are added to the visible things in sacraments, is not superfluous, because one receives determination through the other."*

In a text already quoted S Thomas makes the clear-cut distinction between the two roads which lie before us, and which lead directly to the passion of Christ—an act of the soul, and the use of external things, " actus animae, usus exteriorum rerum." The former is faith, the latter is the sacrament. Let us give this distinction its full value. The " external things " are as solid a road to Christ as the " act of the soul." The sacramental signs, which are the external things alluded to by the Thomistic distinction, have become, in God's Providence, a distinct supernatural world, as real as the supernatural world of the graces given to the souls of men; at the same time, those blessed signs differ radically from the acts of man's soul done under the inspiration of the Holy Ghost. They are things, visible, palpable realities, not breathings of the Spirit in the hearts of men. They are not mere aids to man's memory; they are not only opportune re-

* III, Q. lx, Art. vi ad 1m.

minders of the invisible. " If anyone say that sacraments have been instituted solely for the purpose of fostering faith, let him be anathema."* External things have been taken hold of by God as directly as men's souls have been taken hold of by him. Like this visible planet of ours, the supernatural world of salvation is divided into land and water. The graces of the Holy Ghost are the water; the external things, the sacraments, are the land.

* Trent, Sess. vii.

CHAPTER IV

THE PERFECTION OF SACRAMENTAL SIGNIFICATION

IT would argue feeble loyalty to Catholic thought if the abuse that Protestantism has made of the notion of sacramental signification were to frighten the Catholic theologian, and were to render him timid in proclaiming the marvels of these divine signs. We Catholics, more than anyone else, believe that sacraments are signs, commemorations, monuments of the past. If we neglected to do so, whilst trying to save the kernel of the sacrament, we should be destroying its very nature and making it a thing entirely of the spirit, which would be a passing into the night of Protestantism through another door. The sacraments are signs; let us sing this canticle at all times; they are signs of God; they are most perfect signs because, says S Thomas, they contain and they bring about the very thing they signify. " Sacramenta novae legis simul sunt causae, et signa, et inde est, quod, sicut communiter dicitur, ' efficiunt quod figurant.' Ex quo etiam patet, quod habent perfecte rationem sacramenti, inquantum ordinantur ad aliquid sacrum, non solum per modum signi, sed etiam per modum causae." (" The sacraments of the new law are at the same time causes and signs; and on this account it is said commonly that they bring about what they figure. From this it appears also that they are sacraments in the most perfect sense of the word, because they are related to something sacred, not only under the aspect of sign, but also under the aspect of cause.")* In this they differ profoundly from the sacraments of the Old Law. " The sacraments of the Old Law had no power in themselves by which they might have operated towards the bestowal of justifying grace, but they only signified that faith through which men were justified."† " Nostra autem sacramenta gratiam continent et causant " (" But as for our sacraments they contain grace and cause it ").‡ These pregnant words, as already insinuated in a previous chapter, make Catholicism what it is.

The great signs of God we call sacraments are not only powerful in reminding us of the things of God, they are powerful in making the things of God live again. They are powerful tools or instruments in the hand of God;

* III, Q. lxii, Art. i ad 1m.　† III, Q. lxii, Art. vi.
‡ III, Q. lxi, Art. iv ad 2m.

they are signs which at the same time are tools in the hands of Christ, " who worketh until now." This is the profound Thomistic concept of the sacraments, that they are the *instrumenta Dei* for bringing about supernatural effects, so that they may be truly called containers of grace.

For S Thomas this idea of the tool of God is the concept that unites the role of sign and cause in one. A tool is a cause through its very nature, and a tool may be a sign if it is such as to make it clear to all men that it is apt for the work it is expected to do. Is not the sword an emblem as well as a tool of power ? The man who approaches me with a naked sword proclaims my fate as well as executes it, since the sword is the fittest as well as the most direct instrument of death. " Causa instrumentalis, si sit manifesta, potest dici signum effectus occulti; eo quod non solum est causa, sed etiam quodammodo effectus, inquantum movetur a principali agente " (" An instrumental cause may be called the sign of any hidden result [it brings about], for the reason that it is not only the cause in itself, but it is also in a way an effect, inasmuch as it is handled by the principal actor ").* The man who

* III, Q. lxii, Art. i ad 1m.

handles the naked sword is indeed the principal actor. I am not afraid of a sword not held in a man's grip, nor am I afraid of a human hand without that terrible prolongation of a steel sword; but the man and the sword together are overpowering, both as a cause and a sign. The sword is the token of that result which my enemy who bears down upon me has in view.

But let us leave the gruesome and come to our own brighter sphere of symbols. The waters of Baptism, with the words that go with them, proclaim the phenomenon of purification, of cleansing; by themselves they would only be a vague sign, but those waters and those words, in the last analysis, are poured out by the hand, and are spoken by the mouth of Christ; they are truly his tools, as S Thomas says so constantly; by means of them Christ cleanses most literally, no longer the body, but the soul. " That he might sanctify it, (the Church), cleansing it by the laver of water in the word of life."*

Signification and causation of the spiritual thing, of the mystery of faith, are indissolubly united in the Christian sacrament. If the sacrament were only signification of the spiritual

* Eph. v 26.

thing, it would not rise above the great rites of the Old Law; if, on the contrary, a sacrament were causation only, it would lose at once its historic value; it would be no longer a reviving of the past; it would have nothing to connect it with the great historic event of Christ's death. Is it not the burden of every page of the *Summa* of S Thomas on the sacraments that they are representations of the death of Christ ? Whenever the sacramental doctrine is either falsified or deflected from the traditional concept the cause has been this, that men, who ought to have known better, ceased in one way or another to visualise at the same time the double concept of signification and causation. The two concepts are strictly inseparable in this matter of the sacrament. The sacrament must be cause in such wise as actually to represent the past, the present, and the future; and it must signify in such wise as actually to effect the thing to which it points.

Let me anticipate, for the sake of a clear example. The Eucharist would not be a sacrament if it were not causative, a bringing about again of the mystery of the death of Christ; nor would it be a sacrament if that mystery of the death of Christ thus brought about in the Eucharist were not done under signs and symbols. Let us make an extremely bold hypothesis, for the sake of clearness. If the priest at the altar brought down Christ from heaven in his natural state as a full-grown man, this would not be a sacrament in the least, as it would lack the very essence of the sacrament, representative signification. We can never insist enough on this aspect of the sacramental theology; before all things and above all things we are dealing with signs and symbols, not with things in their own proper nature, *in propria specie*. The Eucharist, being the most perfect sacrament, is more powerfully representative than any other. At no time do we deal in the Eucharist with Christ in his natural condition, *in propria specie*. It might almost be said that if at any moment Christ in his natural condition were to step into the sacramental *processus*, the sacrament at once would be made meaningless. He must be there *in specie aliena* in order to safeguard the veracity of the sacrament as a sign. At the same time the signs and symbols which are the constitutional élements of the sacramental world are things that are powerful in the hand of God. They are his tools; they are like the metal disc of a seal in his hand, which, under the pressure of his omnipotence, makes the mystery of faith to appear in relief, were it even the Body and Blood of Christ.

If we were met by Christ in Person in our churches, such gracious encounters would have nothing in common with what is called the sacramental Presence. His Presence in the sacrament must be truly such that at no time could it be seen otherwise than by the eye of faith. One is justified in saying that it is the very condition of the sacramental Presence to transcend all vision and all experience even of the highest order, because there is really no kind of perceptive power in man, or even in the angel, corresponding to that state of being which is properly the sacramental state.

S Thomas has thought it worth his while to write an article in the seventy-sixth Question on this very subject, whether any eye be capable of seeing the Body of Christ as he is in this sacrament. " The Body of Christ, according to the mode of being which it has in this sacrament, cannot be detected, either by the senses or by imagination, but only through the intellect, which is called the spiritual eye. It is, however, detected by various intellects in various degrees. As the mode of being according to which Christ is in this sacrament is entirely supernatural, Christ is visible to the supernatural intellect only, I mean, the divine intellect; and, as a consequence, to the beatified intellect, either of angel or man, which in a participated brightness of the divine intellect sees the supernatural things in the vision of the divine essence; but as for the intellect of man here on earth, it cannot perceive [the sacramental Presence of Christ] otherwise than by faith, as is the case with all other supernatural things; nor is the angelic intellect capable of seeing it, left to its merely natural resources."*

* III, Q. lxxvi, Art. vii.

CHAPTER V

SACRAMENTAL THOUGHT

THE sacramental world is a new world created by God, entirely different from the world of nature and even from the world of spirits. It would be bad theology to say that in the sacraments we have here on earth modes of spiritual realities which resemble the ways of the angels. We have nothing of the kind. If we spoke with the tongues of angels and men it would not help us in the least to express the sacramental realities. Sacraments are a new creation with entirely new laws. They are " the mystery which has been hidden from eternity in God who created all things: that the manifold wisdom of God may be made known to the principalities and powers in heavenly places through the church."*

The creative power of symbols, the productive efficacy of signs, the incredible resourcefulness of simple things in the hand of God to produce spiritual realities, nay, to reproduce them in

* Eph. iii 9.

their historic setting, this is the sacramental world, and it is profoundly unlike any other world.

There is nothing like the sacraments in heaven or on the earth, and it would be a great disparagement of their character to look upon them as mere veils of more substantial spiritual realities.

They are not veiling anything, but they are complete realities in themselves, existing in their own right; they are not *infima et infirma elementa*, weak and mean shadows of things, but they are the virtue of God and the power of God. " Our bodily eye is prevented from a direct vision of Christ's body through those sacramental species under which it exists, not only as through a kind of cover, as we cannot see whatever is hidden through some bodily veil, but because the body of Christ has no relationship to the medium which surrounds the sacrament."*

Sacraments have a mode of existence of their own, a psychology of their own, a grace of their own. If they are not beings in the sense in which man is a being or an angel is a being, they are beings nevertheless, resembling God's nature very closely. It is, no doubt, a constant

* III, Q. lxxvi, Art. vii ad 1m.

tendency with us to make of the sacraments things easily classified under the ordinary headings of human concepts; yet let us remember that sacramental thought is something quite *sui generis*, and the less anthropomorphism, or even the less spiritism, be introduced into it, the better for our theology. Even a master in Israel may well be astonished at the nature of the sacramental power in giving new life: " Jesus answered and said to him: Amen, amen, I say to thee, unless a man be born again, he cannot see the kingdom of God. Nicodemus saith to him: How can a man be born when he is old ? Can he enter a second time into his mother's womb and be born again ? Jesus answered: Amen, amen, I say to thee, unless a man be born again of water and the Holy Ghost, he cannot enter into the kingdom of God. That which is born of the flesh is flesh: and that which is born of the Spirit is spirit. Wonder not that I said to thee: You must be born again. The Spirit breatheth where he will and thou hearest his voice: but thou knowest not whence he cometh and whither he goeth. So is everyone that is born of the Spirit. Nicodemus answered and said to him: How can these things be done ? Jesus answered and ·said to him: Art thou a master in Israel and knowest not these things ?"*

The sacraments have opened new vistas for human thought, and it is not without spiritual loss that men, no doubt with the best of intentions, speak of them in terms which are applicable only to the natural conditions of man or of angel or of Christ himself. To state the Eucharist, to quote only one sacrament, in phrases which can only be true of Christ's natural life, is to relinquish a whole new world of divine revelation. Sacraments are not substitutes for anything else, they are their own end and justification. They produce their own grace and produce it in a way entirely different from all the other modes of participating in the divine life. " The sacrament," says S Thomas, " is achieved, not through the justice of the man who either gives or receives it, but through the power of God."†

I do not hesitate to transcribe a stiff passage from the *Summa*, which states in terse philosophical language the profound originality of the sacramental concept. " The sacrament of the new law is an instrumental cause of grace; therefore grace is in a sacrament of the new law, not indeed according to a likeness of

* John iii 3-10.   † III, Q. lxviii, Art. viii.

species, as an effect is in an univocal cause; nor is grace in the sacrament of the new law according to any kind of form which is proper, permanent, and proportionate for such an effect, as effects are contained in causes not univocal, as, for instance, the things which are generated are contained in the power of the sun. But grace is contained in the sacrament of the new law according to a certain instrumental power which is in a state of flux, and which is incomplete as a natural being."* To make clear this piece of philosophy, which is truly a golden key to the understanding of the sacramental reality, let us put it more colloquially in the following way: Man begets his own offspring in full similarity of nature—that is to say, the child is as truly man as the father. The sun, which is the centre of heat, light and life, is credited by the scholastic thinker with wonderful power of generating forms of life on our planet. The sun is the true cause of the vegetation in our meadows, but it is not an univocal cause, because the big sun does not beget small suns here on earth; it begets forms of life very different from the constitutional elements of the sun. A sacrament is neither the one nor the other: it causes its effects, not only with utmost dis-

* III, Q. lxii, Art. iii.

similarity, but it causes without any of that permanent, proportionate and appropriate vigour which, say, is in the sun. It has no such permanent and natural fixity of being. If a sacrament were a fixed being in its natural condition, radiating forth grace and life, it would not be a sacrament. With all its realism, according to S Thomas, a sacrament is a power which is a flux, and which is incomplete as a natural being. S Thomas calls it *Virtus, quae est fluens, et incompleta in esse naturae.** I do not apologise to my readers for making this appeal to their speculative power in order to establish the truth which will be such a gain to them if once they master it, that in sacraments we deal with realities which one might call elusive, in the sense that we can never say of any sacrament that it is either Christ or Holy Ghost or angel or man in their natural, personal mode of existence, though we may say of the sacrament that it can be Christ himself, if necessary; but it is not the natural Christ; it is the sacramental Christ, which is a very different proposition.

To sum it all up: our devotion for the sacraments and our love of them will be truest and greatest if we grasp the fact that the kingdom

* III, Q. lxii, Art. iii.

of God may be found truly in those external and insignificant elements because they are the signs of spiritual things, but signs, as we have so often said, full of divine efficacies: " Things of the senses looked upon in their natural being have nothing to do with the cult of the kingdom of God; but the kingdom of God is found in them only because they are signs of spiritual things."*

May it not be said that the radical difference between Catholicism and Protestantism is in this, that Protestantism is blind in the spiritual plane to the things of that middle world which lies between the creature and the uncreated God, the sacramental world, which is neither nature nor divinity, yet which partakes of both. Or again—and this is another way of saying the same thing—Protestantism ignores, at least to a very great extent, the fact that there are acts of sanctification which are not the personal act of man, but which are the sacramental effect. The sacramental world is truly a mystical world in the best sense of the word: it is reality without fixity of being. Any effort we make in order to cultivate sacramental thought will be rewarded with precious fruits in our spiritual life. It will make us into true mystics·

* III, Q. lx, Art. iv ad 2m.

Our dear sacraments are truly a stream of life and light: they are unceasing in their operation; they are more like the great natural powers of radiation discovered by modern science than the solid mass that constitutes the planet. The definition of S Thomas of the sacraments: " a power that is a flux," may remind us of the vision of Ezechiel: " And as for the likeness of the living creatures: their appearance was like that of burning coals of fire, and like the appearance of lamps. This was the vision running to and fro in the midst of the living creatures, a bright fire and lightning going forth from the fire. And the living creatures ran and returned like flashes of lightning."* The sacramental flow is truly the flow of the Blood of Christ: in one way or another every sacrament is the fire of Christ's love when he was dying on the Cross. It will be, perhaps, the most satisfying mode of sacramental thought to visualise the sacraments as mysterious carriers of all the powers that are in Christ's death. " The power of Christ's passion," says S Thomas, " is joined on to us (*copulatur nobis*) through faith and through the sacraments, yet in different ways; for the linking up (*continuatio*) which is through faith takes place through the

* Ezech. i 13, 14.

act of the soul: but the linking up which is through the sacraments takes place through the use of external things."*

Let us bear well in mind this wonderful distinction of S Thomas. Our personal acts link us up with Christ; in this Catholics and Protestants are agreed. But the use of external things, of the sacramental signs, also links us up with Christ, historically as well as actually. This linking up is as great a phenomenon as a linking up by faith, and in this the Catholic has a supreme certainty of approaching Christ which is denied to the Protestant. This linking up of the sacrament with the real Christ on the Cross is understood by S Thomas in a very realistic sense, so much so that according to him the Christian sacrament could not have existed unless Christ himself had existed in historic time. Faith in Christ could exist before Christ appeared in the reality of the flesh: but the Christian sacrament presupposes the natural and historic presence of Christ on earth. The reason is this, that Christ in his flesh is the effective cause of all the powers that are in the Christian sacrament. Now the effective cause must have a real priority of actual existence: "What does not exist in

* III, Q. lxii, Art. vi.

nature cannot put in motion the use of external things " (" Illud quod nondum est in rerum natura, non movet secundum usum exteriorum rerum ").* A mental act, like that of faith, may precede the event; but signs which are full of actual efficacy receive their power from the historic event or person, and therefore imply the important circumstance that the event has taken place, that the person has lived and died.

Sacraments are, then, truly an energy that comes from Christ in person, a radiation from the charity of the Cross, a stream of grace from the pierced side of Christ. " It is manifest, therefore, that the sacraments of the Church have their power more particularly from the passion of Christ, whose efficacy is joined on to us, as it were, through the receiving of the sacraments. As the emblem of this, from the side of Christ hanging on the Cross there flowed water and blood, of which the one belongs to Baptism and the other to the Eucharist, which are the two supreme sacraments."†

* III, Q. lxii, Art. vi.　　　† III, Q. lxii, Art. v.

CHAPTER VI

THE SACRAMENTAL ROLE

WE are all familiar with the theological adage *Sacramenta sunt propter homines*. Sacraments are all for the benefit of man. It is a precious maxim which enables us to steer clear of all rigorisms in the use of sacraments. But the same adage would defeat its own ends, or certainly would defeat the ends of the sacramental system, if it were meant to express an exclusively utilitarian view of the sacrament, though the utility would be, of course, of the spiritual order. No supernatural grace could ever be so one-sided. A grace represents the interests of God as well as the interests of man: it implies the glory of God as well as the salvation of man. We may propound it as a general maxim in the doctrine of grace that man's profit and God's glory are the twofold aspects of one and the same thing, grace. Sacraments would not be the divine things they are if they had not a face turned towards God as well as a face turned towards man.

S Thomas understood this aspect well, and

he has kept his sacramental doctrine quite immune from exclusive spiritual utilitarianism. The sacrament is divine cult quite as much as human purification. Let us quote his words once more: " The sacramental grace seems to be ordained chiefly for two ends: firstly, to remove those gaps (made in the soul) through past sins, inasmuch as sins are past events as acts, though they are permanent things as guilt; and secondly, the sacraments are ordained to render the soul perfect in those things which belong to the worship of God, according to the rite of the Christian life."*

S Thomas goes on to explain that Christ on the Cross destroyed all sin; but that he has also on the Cross instituted the rite of the Christian religion, offering himself as an oblation and victim to God: " Similiter etiam per suam passionem initiavit ritum christianae religionis, offerens seipsum oblationem, et hostiam Deo."† Sacraments consequently represent the Cross in the double aspect of atonement for sin and of worship of God.

It will be readily seen that the introduction of the element of cult into the sacramental system as its second and nobler half, modifies profoundly sacramental thought. The sacra-

* III, Q. lxii, Art. v.   † *Ibid.*

ment, remaining a sacrament, may be a worship as much as a sanctification; in fact, it is more truly a sacrament through the worship of God than through the sanctification of man. If we go back on the fundamental concept of the sacrament, that in one way or another it is a representation of Christ's passion, the element of cult belongs to it intrinsically, as it belonged intrinsically to Christ's death on the Cross, which before all things and above all things was a sacrifice unto God. It would be an easy task to point out this cult side in every one of the sacraments, were we even leaving out, for the moment, the Eucharist. Some sacraments possess the cult side more explicitly than others. S Thomas thinks that the sacraments which imprint a character on the human soul have the cult element more abundantly, always excepting the Eucharist. " Through certain sacraments which imprint a character, man is more especially sanctified through a certain consecration, as being delegated for the purpose of divine worship, as even inanimate things may be said to be sanctified because they are set apart for divine worship."*

In a previous article of the same Question S Thomas has the beautiful words which I

* III, Q. lxiii, Art. vi ad 2m.

quote in their Latin first: " Illi qui deputantur ad cultum christianum, cujus auctor est Christus, characterem accipiunt, quo Christo configurantur " (" Those who are delegated for the Christian cult, whose author is Christ, receive a [sacramental] character, by which they are made conformable to Christ "). *But I need not elaborate this point any longer. The Thomistic view of the sacrament is clear; it unites indissolubly cult and sanctification; it prepares us for the idea of the Christian sacrifice, which is highest worship, being found in a sacrament, as sacraments are cult, not by a kind of after-thought, but through their first and most conspicuous element. Everyone will easily see what broad deflection it would mean in the sacramental concept if at any time we turned entirely to the left, so to speak, to the element of sanctification, forgetting all about the element of cult. Let us cling to the dear old maxim *Sacramenta propter homines*, provided we understand that nothing is so useful to man as to adore God. If we let man have the sacraments plentifully, without any stint, it is in order to enable him, before all things and above all things, to do the works of the Christian cult, so that he be never short of the things

* III, Q. lxiii, Art. iii ad 2m.

48

of the Christian rite, but that he have them at his disposal every morning as the sun rises.

It ought to be an habitual thought with us that the sacrament is a *res sacra*—a sacred thing —given to man so as to enable him to approach God. It is the cup of sacrificial blood which man holds in his hand so that he may have the right of entering into the holy of holies. Man is active in the sacramental system, not only passive; in it he gives back to God God's own gifts. I do not speak here of such acts as may be necessary on the part of man to make him a fit recipient of the sacrament: such acts are more truly called dispositions or predisposi- tions. I am now alluding to the real sacra- mental activity of which S Thomas speaks so much. " The sacrament belongs to the divine cult in a threefold manner; firstly, by way of the action; secondly, by way of the agent; thirdly, by way of the recipient. By way of action itself, the Eucharist belongs to the divine cult because in that sacrament divine cult is found in a supreme manner, as it is the sacrifice of the Church. . . . As for agents in the sacra- ments, we have the sacrament of Order, because through this sacrament men are delegated to deliver the sacrament unto other men; for recipients, however, we have the sacrament of

Baptism, because through this man gets the power of receiving the other sacraments of the Church. This is why Baptism is called the gate of all the sacraments. To this latter class also belongs the sacrament of Confirmation."* In all this we clearly perceive the tendency of the theology of S Thomas. Sacraments are activities, even on the part of man, because they are either the divine cult itself, or man's sanctification for the divine cult. It would certainly be a poor sacramental system if in it man were merely passive, were nothing but a recipient; the sacrament would lack the fire of life, the exhilaration of giving.

Before entering into the heart of our subject we ought to examine the special function of sacramental grace in the organism of human sanctity. "The sacramental grace," says S Thomas, " adds to grace commonly so called, and above the virtues and gifts, a certain divine help, in order to enable man to reach the goal of the sacraments, so that the sacramental grace adds something above the grace of virtues and gifts."† S Thomas makes the sacramental grace a kind of species under a larger genus of grace: " Ratio sacramentalis gratiae se habet ad gratiam communiter dictam, sicut ratio speciei

* III. Q. lxiii, Art. vi.   † III, Q. lxii, Art. ii.

ad genus."* Let us bear in mind, above all things, the individual character of each sacrament. There is no overlapping in their activities; there is no confusion in their respective roles; they are not interchangeable in their purpose; they are as completely different in their spiritual results as they are different in their external symbols. The water of Baptism, the bread and wine of the Eucharist, and the chrism of Confirmation are very different elements indeed, but they are not more different than the internal results of their respective sacramental power.

The sacramental graces are profoundly modified through their intimate connection with Christ's passion and death. They are not grace absolutely, but grace as flowing from the pierced side of Christ. Why is it, asks S Thomas, that Baptism washes away, even in the old sinner who approaches it, every stain of sin and all the guilt of sin besides? " The suffering of the passion of Christ is communicated to the one who is baptised, inasmuch as he becomes a member of Christ, as if he himself (the baptised man) had suffered that pain, and therefore all his sins are remitted through the pain of Christ's passion."†

* III, Q. lxii, Art. ii ad 3m.   † III, Q. lxix, Art. ii.

Another terse phrase from the same place: " It is clear, then, that to every one who is baptised the passion of Christ is communicated for a remedy as if he himself had suffered and had died " (" Ex quo patet, quod omni baptizato communicatur passio Christi ad remedium, ac si ipse passus et mortuus esset "). Could sacramental grace be stated in a more glorious phrase ? The privilege of the baptised man is " ac si ipse passus et mortuus esset."

CHAPTER VII

THE SACRAMENTAL SETTING OF THE EUCHARIST

WE need not regret having spent our first efforts in trying to master the salient points of the sacramental doctrine of the Church. Nothing could be more futile than an attempt to enter into the understanding of the Christian Eucharist without this previous education in the broader concepts of the sacramental idea. The Eucharist is a sacrament; it is nothing but a sacrament; and it is set like a jewel in the very midst of the sacramental marvel. *Tantum ergo sacramentum veneremur cernui* is the most popular, as well as the most technically exact, expression of Catholic admiration for the great gift of the Eucharist; we lie prostrate before the sacrament in our churches and cathedrals.

It is certainly a great merit of S Thomas that he has found it possible to give an absolutely complete theology of the Eucharist without ever departing one moment from the sacramental concept. He lays the foundations of sacramental theology in general in so broad a fashion that at no time is he compelled to buttress up the glories of any of the seven sacraments through outside considerations, through speculations or theories which have nothing to do with the sacramental notion. High as the sacrament may soar, it soars up from the common sacramental foundation. The blessed Eucharist reaches the very Throne of God as it is the Lamb of God in a state of immolation; it is more than the food of the soul giving immortality; it is the blood of the new covenant; it is the sacrifice of the Lamb unspotted; but all these splendours, unexpected as they may seem, do not take S Thomas by surprise; they are still the sacrament; they can be stated in sacramental terms, and the Eucharist in its double aspect of cult and food, of sacrifice and communion, is not a different sacrament from the other six sacraments, but it is the sacrament *par excellence*. It is the first of the sacraments, not because it goes at any point beyond the divine circle of sacramental significance, but because it rises to the Throne of God from within that great circle. " The Eucharist is the perfect sacrament of the Lord's passion inasmuch as it contains the very Christ himself who suffered " (" Eucharistia est sacramentum perfectum Dominicae passionis, tanquam continens ipsum Christum passum ").*

We make a difference in the Eucharist between the sacrifice and the communion; we do even say that the laity, when they receive communion, receive the sacrament, thus introducing into Eucharistic language a distinction between the Eucharist as sacrifice and the Eucharist as sacrament, which we may accept as an easily workable phrase. Even S Thomas, with his great hold of the oneness of the Eucharistic sacrament, uses this duality of expression when necessary, and distinguishes within the sacrament between sacrifice and sacrament. I shall have to say a word or two on this presently, but let it be clear at once that this is merely a necessity of language, which has nothing in common with the much more drastic divisions of sacrifice and sacrament which were introduced at a later date. But it would be truly disastrous if at any time we came to look upon the Eucharist in its sacrificial aspect as something less sacramental or even non-sacramental, leaving the sacramental denomination exclusively to the reception of Christ's Body and Blood. This would at once remove the Eucharistic sacrifice from the sacramental theory

* III, Q. lxxiii, Art. v ad 2m.

of the Church; it would make of it something
for which there are no provisions in our general
theology. This would set it apart, as a thing
all by itself, with no universal idea to explain
it and to hold it in the general scheme of sanctification. S Thomas would have been the very
last man to make such a blunder; for him, and
in fact for the whole age in which he lived
and taught, the Eucharistic sacrifice is an
essentially sacramental thing; the Eucharist is
a sacrament at its best because it is a ritual
offering up to God in the new covenant. At
no time did S Thomas in his explanation of the
Christian sacrifice go outside his general theory
of the sacraments. In order to explain sacrifice
he never borrows considerations from other
realms of theology; the sacramental theology
provides him with a key to the mystery of the
Mass. We may make this more clear by comparing the conduct of S Thomas with some of
the later theologians. Holding by faith the fact
that at Mass the Son of God is offered up
under the appearance of bread and wine, theologians have asked themselves the question,
How is Christ in a state of victim on the altar?
They have sought for various theories in order
to explain this state of immolation; they have
said, for instance, that Christ's mode of existing

under the Eucharistic species represents a sort of abasement or humiliation compared with his natural state of glory. I do not pretend to criticise such views; I do not deny that the state of abasement may be a state of sacrifice; all that I intend to make clear now is this, that such an explanation of the Eucharistic sacrifice comes not from the centre of the sacramental doctrine, but has been brought in from quite another realm of Christian thought; it has been borrowed from the ethical realm. Humiliation or exaltation are not sacramental notions, but ethical notions. The sacrament is a representation of an historic fact, not an ethical deed which has new meritoriousness. At no time did S Thomas leave the straight road of sacramental thought in all his loving considerations of the Eucharistic mystery. This is true of him when he considers the Eucharist exclusively from the angle of the ritual sacrifice. Having once grasped the profound fact that the Eucharist is a true sacrament, he never lets go of that idea, and he succeeds in giving us a theology of the Eucharist which is a masterpiece of harmonious thought; he places the sacrament of the altar in the centre of the whole sacramental system, and he makes all the other sacraments converge towards it.

We are well aware of the disruption of this harmony at the Reformation, when Protestants denied the sacrificial character of the Eucharist, making of it the merely passive sacrament of receiving the Body and Blood of Christ. I speak now of Protestantism in its early and less antagonistic period of thought, when it still held the Real Presence. It became practically necessary then for the Catholic theologians to distinguish in the Eucharist itself between the sacrament and the sacrifice, reserving the term " sacrament " almost exclusively to the receiving of Holy Communion; but this is merely a tactical move which need not deceive us Catholics; the term " sacrament " covers the whole Eucharist as with a golden baldachino of glory; the sacrifice of the Church, Mass, is truly the sacrament at its best and fullest; and the sacrifice of Mass, if it has any human explanation, must be explained in sacramental concepts.

This is the great work which S Thomas did, a stroke of genius whose importance is not always appreciated by men even of sincere intentions, yet whose effects are great beyond calculation in the past and future history of theology. The Corpus Christi liturgy sings the glory of the divine sacrifice in sacramental terms, and it is certain that the practical treatment by the Church of her divine treasure, the Eucharistic sacrifice, is the sacramental treatment; the divine sacrifice is a thing which is used by man in the human way, as all the other sacraments; it is put at our disposal with lavish abundance.

It is the main scope of this little book to make this idea clear, that in dealing with the Eucharist in all its aspects we are still dealing with a sacrament. The rules that govern its use, its frequency, shall I say, its proprietary rights, are sacramental rules. In the following chapters we shall let S Thomas speak for himself; this present chapter is intended to state the position which I am taking up. It will be easy for anyone to perceive at a glance that to restrict explanations of the Eucharistic mystery, and, above all, of the Eucharistic sacrifice, to sacramental concepts, is in a way a limitation of the scope of imagination, and shall I say, of devotional exaggeration? Yet let us be quite sure of one thing, that the Eucharist, in all its magnitude, is a very definite thing, as all sacraments are definite things, at no time rendering superfluous any of the other elements of the Christian dispensation.

Three concepts belonging to the general

theory of sacraments in the theology of S Thomas, more than any others, have made it possible for him to keep the Eucharist entirely within the sacramental circle. Here I am repeating what we have already said in a previous chapter. The first concept, so prolific in its consequences, is the representative significance of every sacrament as a past, a present, and a future; the past being the death of Christ on the cross, the present being the very thing which the external symbol signifies, the future being the union with Christ in glory. The second concept, belonging to the sacraments in general, and also fertile in endless results, is this, that the sacrament is not only man's healing but also God's glorification, the cult of God. It is readily perceived that the Eucharistic sacrifice which is radically a representative sacrifice of a past immolation, and which is essentially a supreme act of worship, moves easily within such broad views concerning sacraments in general. The third idea so familiar to S Thomas is this, that the sacrament contains what it signifies; that it is not merely an external symbol, but a true carrier of its spiritual realities. This notion of containing, to which S Thomas clings with such tenacity in his general theory on the sacraments, makes it possible for him to speak of the immolated Christ as being contained in the sacrament. " The sacrament is called a victim (*hostia*) because it contains Christ himself, who is the victim of salvation."*

S Thomas calls the Eucharist the sacrament *per antonomasiam.*† Antonomasia, we may well explain with the Standard Dictionary, is a figure of speech whereby an epithet stands for a proper name, or one individual for a whole species, as incorporating in itself alone the qualities that are to be found all over the species. I cannot resist quoting more fully from this same place in the *Summa*, where S Thomas shows all the skill of an expert grammarian in explaining the various names given to the Eucharist by Catholic tradition. By doing so, I shall incidentally bring forward a passage which is a very clear statement of the representative character of the Eucharist, which, as I said a moment ago, is the first of the three decisive concepts common to the Eucharist and to the sacraments in general.

An objector said that most of the names which old usage appropriates to the Eucharist might also be applied to other sacraments, and

* III, Q. lxxiii, Art. iv ad 3m.
† III, Q. lxxiii, Art. iv ad 2m.

that, consequently, they are not characteristic of the Eucharist. All sacraments of the New Law, he says, are a good grace (*bona gratia*), so they might all be called a Eucharist; all sacraments help us on the road of life, so they might all be called a viaticum; all sacraments achieve something sacred, so they might all be called sacrifice; in all the sacraments the faithful come together, so they all might be called communion; why, then, reserve the term of Eucharist, of viaticum, of sacrifice, of communion, to one sacrament alone ? Thus far the objector. To this S Thomas replies, as already insinuated, that whatever is common to all the other sacraments is predicated of this sacrament through antonomasia, on account of its excellency. " Ad secundum dicendum, quod id quod est commune omnibus sacramentis, attribuiter antonomastice huic propter ejus excellentiam."*

A more telling way there could not be of stating that the Eucharist in all its aspects must remain within the sacramental circle; but let us hear the main doctrine contained in this same article: " This sacrament has a threefold signification; one with respect to the past as far as it is commemorative of the Lord's passion,

* III, Q. lxxiii, Art. iv ad 2m.

which was a true sacrifice as said above, and according to this it is called a sacrifice; it has a second signification with regard to a present thing, I mean ecclesiastical oneness, into which men are received through the sacrament, and according to that aspect it is called communion. . . . It has a third signification with regard to the future, inasmuch as the sacrament is a figure of the fruition of God which will take place in heaven, and according to this aspect it is called viaticum, because it gives us here on earth the means of getting there. According to this aspect also it is called Eucharist, which means ' good grace,' because the grace of God is eternal life.''* If this is a broad and comprehensive view of the Eucharist it is not broader nor more comprehensive than the general view of sacramental grace held by S Thomas. The difference is not in breadth or width, but in height and depth. *Propter ejus excellentiam* things are simply truer in the case of the Eucharist, and if in a well-known colloquialism blood is thicker than water, the Eucharistic reality within the sacramental vessel is more effective because it is Blood, the Blood of God himself.

* III, Q. lxxiii, Art. iv.

CHAPTER VIII

SACRAMENTAL HARMONY

WHAT we have to say in this chapter is entirely for Catholics, for those who believe all the Church teaches on the holy Eucharist and on the sacraments generally. The line of argumentation followed is wholly *ad hominem*, an appeal to those very truths which we hold dear.

With most Catholics their knowledge and their appreciation of the Eucharist is in a way clearer and more pronounced than their knowledge and appreciation of the great sacramental system of the Church considered as a whole. The reason of this preference in favour of the Eucharist is obvious. In nothing are we more carefully instructed than in the things of the Eucharist; first communions are almost a social feature in modern Catholicism. Of course this is all to the good, and it is my purpose now to make use of that charisma of our own days, love of the Eucharist, in order to give the sacramental doctrine of the Church, con-

64

sidered in its more universal aspect, the benefit of our devotion.

The Eucharist ought really to illuminate for us all the other sacraments with its own radiance. The Eucharist is the queen amongst the seven sisters of grace, the Catholic sacraments. Is there not sometimes on the one hand a danger of giving the Eucharist a position such as would hardly retain it in its sacramental setting, whilst, on the other hand, there is perhaps a greater peril of our lowering the status of the other sacraments to conventional forms of small spiritual power? The Eucharist, then, ought to save for us the spiritual glories of all the other sacraments, and keep them for us within the orbit of the divine Presence, whilst the sacraments which do not contain the Body and Blood of Christ, and yet are sacraments truly so called, will, for their part, enable us to see even the Eucharist in its true perspective.

We may, then, put it in the following way: One sacrament, whilst remaining a sacrament entirely, and through the very laws of its sacramentality, and not as a kind of unusual feature or external adjunct, contains the true Body and the true Blood of Christ; it does this in virtue of its sacramental state, not because it is more than a sacrament. So we turn to the other

65

sacraments and say: If a sacrament may be the Body and Blood of Christ, can we be surprised at anything that may be said of any of the other sacraments ? After all, they are sacraments in the truest and most literal sense of the word, not in a diminished way, not in an apologetic form of spiritual power; they are all of them the seven spirits of God, sent out over the whole world. Good traditional Catholicism loves to keep the seven together, as one family, and the Council of Trent has given them all letters patent of nobility. " If anyone says . . . that any of these seven is not truly and properly a sacrament, let him be anathema."* There is among the seven a diversity in that which the Council calls dignity, one or the other sacrament possessing greater nobility inside the same nature. " If anyone says . . . that in no wise one sacrament is more worthy than another, let him be anathema."†

The supreme sacrament is, of course, the blessed Eucharist. S Thomas calls it simply *Potissimum inter alia sacramenta.* Yet his way of explaining this supremacy of the Eucharist shows clearly how well he understood the whole sacramental system to be one perfect

* Trent, Sess. vii, Canon i.
† *Ibid.*, Canon iii.

66

organism, where the seven arteries of life work in unison. He sees a threefold reason for the supremacy of the Eucharist: "In it Christ is contained substantially, whilst in the other sacraments there is a certain instrumental power derived from Christ" ("Nam in sacramento Eucharistiae continetur ipse Christus substantialiter; in aliis autem sacramentis continetur quaedam virtus instrumentalis participata a Christo").* Again, all the other sacraments prepare men for the Eucharist, and find in it their consummation. Thirdly—and this is the ritual aspect of the sacraments—Catholic practice makes the other sacraments end in the celebration of the Eucharist. "Tertio hoc apparet ex ritu sacramentorum: nam fere omnia sacramenta in Eucharistia consummantur, ut Dionysius dicit."†

Without being hypercritical and without finding fault with the ways in which other men think, may I not venture a mild censure of much that is written with a sincere intention of instructing the people of God? We seem to have isolated the Eucharist, making it stand like a cedar of Lebanon in solitary grandeur on the mountain-top, when, with all its wonderful fruitfulness, it is only one of the trees of

* III, Q. lxv, Art. iii.　　　　　　† *Ibid.*

the supernatural Eden of God. It occupies the centre; it is surrounded by the six trees that bear fruit unto eternal life, but it is not a solitary growth of disproportionate size. We shall understand the Eucharist better if we know much about the other sacraments, and we shall also be taught by the supreme marvel, the Eucharist, how to accept the other marvels which are its companions.

Even masters in theology have not seen, as they ought to have seen, the true harmony of the sacramental system; they accept everything the Church teaches about the Eucharist, about Transubstantiation, about the power of the priest at the altar; they could not refuse the obedience of faith to such doctrines, which embody the intense objective reality of the sacrament of the altar; but for various reasons, which are not relevant to our subject, such men, when they come to the other sacraments, practically reduce them to infallible signs of grace, denying to them those qualities of life and power which they have to grant to the Eucharist. This attitude is, of course, extremely illogical. Anyone who believes in the Eucharist, as every Catholic theologian does, grants enough to the external thing in the supernatural sphere, the sign, to make him ready for more. If under the appearance of bread and wine there can be the Body and the Blood of Christ, S Thomas, the most honest and logical of all thinkers, will say that under baptismal water there also can be the power of the Holy Ghost, so that baptismal water, or any other sacramental sign, is not only an infallible token of God's activity in the souls of men, but that it is more: the water, the chrism, and the words of absolution, they all contain a participated power from Christ.

"Is the Eucharist a sacrament?" asks S Thomas. "As the power of the Holy Ghost is with regard to the water of Baptism, so the true body of Christ is with regard to the appearance of bread and wine; and therefore the appearances of bread and wine effect nothing except through the power of Christ's true body " (" Sicut autem se habet virtus Spiritus Sancti ad aquam baptismi, ita se habet corpus Christi verum ad speciem panis, et vini; unde species panis, et vini non efficiunt aliquid, nisi virtute corporis Christi veri ").*

There is, then, a close relationship between the power of the baptismal water and the power of the sacramental bread; there is truly no abyss between sacrament and sacrament.

* III, Q. lxxiii, Art. i ad 2m.

The whole sacramental efficiency in the theology of S Thomas receives wonderful unity through the doctrine of the supernatural instrumentality. All the sacraments, not excepting the Eucharist, considered at least as communion, are like divine tools in the hands of Christ; with them he profoundly stirs the world of souls, and raises it up to the level of God.

"How is it," asks an objector, "that the sacrament, in which Christ is received after all *sub specie aliena*, under a foreign form, is still capable of bringing man to the possession of Christ *in specie propria*, in the proper form, in heavenly glory?" Answer: "That Christ should be received under a foreign form belongs to the very nature of the sacrament which acts instrumentally. Now nothing prevents an instrumental cause from producing an effect which is superior" ("Hoc quod Christus sub aliena specie sumitur, pertinet ad rationem sacramenti, quod instrumentaliter agit. Nihil autem prohibet, causam instrumentalem producere potiorem effectum").* The Eucharist, though it contain the very Body and the very Blood of Christ, is still an instrumental causality with respect to eternal glory; and this is the very definition, according to S Thomas, of the

* III, Q. lxxix, Art. ii ad 3m.

whole sacramental causality: it is instrumental in the hands of God. The sacramental thing, the sign and the word, receives from God all such energies and precisions for operation as an artist puts into the tool with which he carves a statue. In this S Thomas finds the superiority of the sacrament of the New Law to the sacrament of the Old Law.

The three sacramental characters, again, of Baptism, Confirmation, and Holy Order, are, in the eyes of S Thomas, psychic instrumentalities through which God operates inside the sacramental system, making the sacrament produce the sacrament.

The official minister of the sacrament is merely an instrument of God. " The ministers of the Church do not cleanse men who come to the sacraments, and they do not give grace in their own power, but Christ in his power does it through them, as through certain instruments, and therefore the effect follows, in those who receive the sacrament, not unto the likeness of the ministers, but into a configuration with Christ."* By making sacramental ministry another form of divine instrumentality, S Thomas has pulled together the whole sacramental system into an indissoluble complex of divine

* III, Q. lxiv, Art. v ad 1m.

71.

vitality. He is far indeed from that loosely connected and almost disjointed theology of the sacrament which is not an uncommon phenomenon in our days.

The difference between the Eucharist and the other sacraments is, of course, clear to the mind of S Thomas; but he states it again sacramentally, not in phrases borrowed from the natural order of things. " A sacrament is that which contains something sacred. A thing may be sacred in a twofold manner, either absolutely, or with reference to something else. Now this is the difference between the Eucharist and the other sacraments which have a matter known to the senses, that the Eucharist contains something sacred absolutely, I mean Christ himself; but the water of Baptism contains something sacred with regard to something else,—that is to say, it contains the power of sanctifying; and the same thing may be said of the chrism and of the other sacramental things. Therefore the sacrament of the Eucharist is fully accomplished (*perficitur*) in the very consecration of matter, whilst the other sacraments are fully accomplished in the application of the matter to the man to be sanctified. From this another difference follows; for in the sacrament of the Eucharist what is the ' thing and the sacrament ' is in the matter itself; but what is the 'thing' only—I mean the grace which is given—is in the one who receives the Eucharist; but in Baptism both are in the recipient, that is to say, character, which is the 'thing and the sacrament' and the grace of remission of sins, which is the 'thing' only, and the same may be said of the other sacraments."* This passage is of extreme importance in sacramental matters; every theologian ought to know it by heart; nothing better has been said in the course of centuries on the unity of the sacramental system, with its diversity of dignity. The fundamental principle, that the Eucharist is fully with us, is completely performed through the consecration of the matter, is the basis of all we have to say on the sacramental aspect of Mass; the consecration is, of course, the complete Eucharist already, because it is the complete memory of Christ's passion.

I must say a few words, however, before ending this chapter, on the theological distinction here made use of by S Thomas, which runs through his whole sacramental doctrine.

The ancient theologians with S Thomas have this threefold division, *sacramentum tantum*, the sacrament only, *sacramentum et res*, the sacra-

* III, Q. lxxiii, Art. i ad 3m.

ment and the thing, *res tantum*, the thing only.

The first, *sacramentum*, is all that we know as the signification, with its divine power and its commemorative affinities. The ' sacrament and the thing ' is the spiritual inwardness of the whole sacramental signification and no longer the external symbolism. Thus in Baptism the character which is distinct from all the other spiritual results of Baptism would be called by S Thomas *sacramentum et res*, because baptismal character, an entirely spiritual result of the external rite, is still a sacramental thing, because in its turn it is a representation of, and a configurement with, the sacerdotal office of Christ, as will be said later. ' Sacrament and thing ' thus holds a very important position in the old theology. It is a blending of the internal spiritual reality, *res*, with signification, *sacramentum*. Very logically, then, does S Thomas declare the fact in the above passage that in the Eucharist ' sacrament and thing ' is in the external matter itself, because truly the ' thing,' the spiritual reality, the Body and Blood of Christ, under the appearance of bread and wine, is also ' sacrament '—that is, representative in a new way of the Christ on the cross, when Body and Blood were separated.

SACRAMENTAL HARMONY

S Thomas admits really a double signification in the sacraments—at least, in some of them; first, the external thing signifies; and then the internal, spiritual reality, immediately produced by the sacrament, has, in its turn, the role of representation. The Eucharist excels, because in it *sacramentum et res* is not in the recipient, but in the external signs of bread and wine. Here, again, we have a truly sacramental basis for the sacrificial aspect of the Eucharist.

Coming now to the *res*—the ' thing '—it would not be accurate reading of the old masters to say that by it is meant grace in general. What is meant is specific, sacramental grace, such as spiritual regeneration in Baptism, such as the union of charity in the Eucharist, when the faithful receive it in communion.

The middle member of the threefold division is really the most interesting to the theologian, because it means a transposing of sacramental signification into the first spiritual results of the sacrament. For the Eucharist it means that not only the whole external rite of Mass signifies sacrifice, but the consecrated elements, or rather, the infinitely holy Thing under the elements, also signifies sacrifice, as being the immediate representation of Christ immolated on the cross.

CHAPTER IX

A CRITICAL STUDY OF S THOMAS

THE present chapter is intended to redeem the promise made in a previous one to let S Thomas speak for himself. We said that the great Doctor found it possible to state the whole Eucharistic mystery in sacramental concepts. That he did so we now proceed to show. There is this very evident fact that nowhere has S Thomas treated the *sacrificium Missæ* as a separate theological matter; in this he stands in striking contrast to later theologians. The Eucharistic sacrifice is entirely subsumed under the concept of the Eucharistic sacrament—nay, more, the Eucharistic sacrament is said by him to have its main expression and celebration in the consecration, which consecration, again, according to him, is the direct and complete sacramental representation of Christ's passion, and as such, is sacrifice.

It will be a simple task to put before the reader a number of evident texts from the *Summa*. There is, first of all, the never-varied habit of S Thomas of making the term *sacra-*

mentum the subject of every phrase that has anything to do with the Eucharist. He will say that the sacrament is sacrifice; that the sacrament is celebrated at Mass; that to receive the sacrament in communion is a natural outcome of the sacrament; he will even say that the sacrament is at the same time sacrament and sacrifice; sacrament when it is received, sacrifice when it is offered up, giving us an apparently difficult grammatical poser, which reminds one of a schoolboy's definition of man, when he said that man consists of man and woman. There is no irreverence intended in this, as we are dealing with an arduous subject, in which difficulties of expression make children of us all. When S Thomas says that the sacrament is at the same time sacrament and sacrifice he is far from that modern duality which divides the Eucharist into two separate realities: his very phrase implies the containing of two things in one—nay, even the containing of a minor thing in a greater thing; the sacrifice is the greater thing which contains the minor thing, the participation. But of this more presently.

Let us see how the word *sacramentum* is the subject for everything that is being predicated of the Eucharist, be it sacrifice or be it communion.

An objector says that this sacrament of the Eucharist ought not to be of profit to anyone except the one who receives it, for the sacrament is of the same kind with the other sacraments: but the other sacraments are of profit only to the one who receives them; the effect of Baptism, for instance, is exclusively for the baptised subject. Therefore this sacrament, too, ought to be considered as being unto profit only for the one who receives it; so far the objector. The answer of S Thomas is simple and limpid. " The reply is that this sacrament in preference to the other sacraments possesses this, that it is a sacrifice, and so there is a difference of condition " (" Dicendum quod hoc sacramentum prae aliis habet, quod est sacrificium; et ideo non est similis ratio ").*

To the objector who finds it difficult to reconcile completeness of the sacrament with the Latin usage of communicating under one kind only, S Thomas replies that the perfection of the sacrament is not in the use made of it by the faithful, but in the consecration of the matter; for the representation of Christ's passion is performed in the very consecration of the sacrament: " Perfectio hujus sacramenti non est in usu fidelium, sed in consecratione materiae.

* III, Q. lxxix, Art. vii ad 1m.

78

. . . Representatio Dominicae passionis agitur in ipsa consecratione hujus sacramenti, in qua non debet corpus sine sanguine consecrari."*

The sacrament, for S Thomas, is essentially in the consecration; which, again, is essentially the representation of Christ's passion and therefore sacrifice, as Body and Blood are consecrated separately. Speaking of the celebration of Mass, S Thomas says that it matters little whether the sacrament be consecrated by one or many, provided the rite of the Church be observed.†

There is another very clear identification of sacrament and sacrifice. Mass, for S Thomas, is simply the sacrament which is being celebrated: " In mass there are two things to be considered, namely the sacrament itself, which is the principal thing, and the prayers for the living and the dead which are said at mass. From the point of view, then, of sacrament, the mass of a bad priest is not of less value than the mass of a good priest, because in both cases the same sacrament is being performed " (" Quantum ergo ad sacramentum, non minus valet missa sacerdotis mali, quam boni, quia utrobique idem conficitur sacramentum ").‡ To offer up Mass for S Thomas is simply *conficere*

* III, Q. lxxx, Art. xii ad 2m et 3m.
† III, Q. lxxxii, Art. ii.   ‡ III, Q. lxxxii, Art. vi.

sacramentum, to make the sacrament, in the terse but perfectly exact language of the Catholic theologians of the period.

Nothing would be easier for me than to multiply texts of that kind, gleaned from all over the *Summa* of S Thomas, where he treats of the sacraments and particularly of the Eucharist. All such texts are *obiter dicta,* casual remarks for the most part, which show how firmly the idea was imbedded in the mind of S Thomas that the celebration of Mass is a sacramental act, and that, in a cherished phrase of his, the Eucharist is celebrated in the consecration more truly than in the communion: " The sacrament is accomplished (*perficitur*) in the consecration of the matter; the use of the sacrament by the faithful does not of necessity belong to the sacrament, but is something following upon the sacrament " (" Hoc sacramentum perficitur in consecratione materiae: usus autem fidelium non est de necessitate sacramenti, sed est aliquid consequens ad sacramentum ").*

It may be that our minds to-day are less habituated to the view that the Eucharistic sacrament is chiefly the offering of the sacrifice of Mass; yet there can be no doubt that such

* III, Q. lxxiv, Art. vii.

was the attitude of mind in the ages of faith, of which S Thomas is the finest representative. Communion is held by him to be something that follows upon a sacramental act which is already complete, I mean the communion of the faithful, as distinguished from the communion of the priest at Mass. " The use of the consecrated matter in the Eucharist belongs to a certain perfection of the sacrament, just as operation is not the first, but the second perfection of a thing " ("Ad quamdam perfectionem sacramenti pertinet materiae consecratae usus, sicut operatio non est prima, sed secunda perfectio rei ").* The simile borrowed from philosophy is very telling. Operation is said to be the second perfection of a thing; S Thomas means that a man is perfect man, in the first instance, for having a nature; to think and act with that human nature is the second perfection; yet man is man fully, even when he does not actually think or work. So the Eucharist is sacrament fully the moment it is consecrated. It fulfils its mission then, because it is completely sacrament, being a sacrifice.

Another beautiful and terse phrase which I cannot resist quoting as the last selection is the following: " Usus autem sacramenti est

* III, Q. lxxviii, Art. i ad 2m.

consequenter se habens ad hoc sacramentum."*
The use of the sacrament follows the sacrament,
is the meaning of S Thomas. In modern
words we should say communion follows
Mass; but who does not see how much more
accurate is the phrase of S Thomas? The
sacrament has already existed, has accomplished
its great mission, has fulfilled its role, before
the faithful approach to receive it; shall we say
that the faithful come in at the end of the sacred
drama? The sacrament has been completed,
has shed its light heavenwards and earthwards,
before the faithful eat it, because the sacrifice
has taken place once more. If sacrifice and
sacrament were not identical, how could it ever
be said that the use of the sacrament comes
after the sacrament?

When S Thomas comes to distinguish between
the various effects of the great sacrament, then,
for the first time, he makes a less precise distinction and talks in a less definite fashion, as
already mentioned. He says: " This sacrament
is at the same time sacrifice and sacrament; but
it has the nature of sacrifice inasmuch as it is
offered up, and it has the nature of a sacrament
inasmuch as it is partaken " (" Hoc sacramentum simul est sacrificium, et sacramentum:

* III, Q. lxxxii, Art. iv ad 2m.

sed rationem sacrificii habet, inquantum offertur; rationem autem sacramenti, inquantum sumitur ").*

This easy distinction has often been adopted, and it is made use of with great effect by so orthodox a manual as the Catechism of the Council of Trent. But the whole phraseology of S Thomas forbids our confining the sacramental character of the Eucharist exclusively to the *sumptio*. S Thomas does not say the Eucharist is sacrament and sacrifice, but he says " this sacrament is sacrament and sacrifice "; the one and the same sacrament has a twofold function, the more common sacramental function of feeding the soul, in which function it resembles all the other sacraments, and which, therefore, may be called directly sacramental; and the sacrament has the function of sacrifice, which is a property exclusive to the Eucharist, and which it is quite legitimate to distinguish from the ordinary function of spiritual feeding without losing in any way its own innate sacramentality.

Let us conclude this study of the mind of S Thomas with a more lengthy passage from the seventy-third Question, sixth Article, which, besides clinching the matter as to what I might

* III, Q. lxxix, Art. v.

well call the Eucharistic grammar of S Thomas, will be a devotional ending to our critical survey.

S Thomas sets out to show that the Paschal lamb of the Old Law was the most perfect figure of the Eucharistic sacrament. " In this sacrament we may keep in mind three things, what is ' sacrament ' only, namely bread and wine; what is the ' thing and the sacrament,' namely the true body of Christ; and what is the ' thing ' only, I mean the effect of the sacrament (on man's soul). Considering what is ' sacrament ' only, the most perfect figure of this sacrament was the offering by Melchisedech, who offered up bread and wine. But looking at Christ in his passion (*Christum passum*) who is contained in this sacrament, the figures of it are all the sacrifices of the old Testament, chiefly the sacrifice of expiation, which was the most solemn. Coming now to the effect of the sacrament, its principal type was the manna which had in it ' all that is delicious, and the sweetness of every taste,' as it is said in the sixteenth chapter of Wisdom, just as the grace of this sacrament refreshes the soul in every way. The Paschal lamb, however, was the figure of the sacrament according to all those three aspects. According to the first aspect, because it was eaten with unleavened bread. . . . According to the second aspect, because it was offered up by the whole multitude of the children of Israel on the fourteenth day of the month, and this was the figure of Christ's passion, who on account of his innocence is called the Lamb. According to the effect, moreover, because through the blood of the Paschal lamb the children of Israel were protected from the destroying angel, and were brought forth from the slavedom of Egypt: for this reason, then, the Paschal lamb is considered to be the chief figure of the sacrament, because it represents it in every aspect."*

Not once in this copious passage does S Thomas hesitate to make the word " sacrament " the subject of which so many varied things are being predicated. We may rest assured that we shall be speaking good Catholic language in preferring to all other terms the term of sacrament, when we speak of the blessed Eucharist. The prayer of the Church comes naturally to our lips: " Deus, qui nobis sub sacramento mirabili passionis tuae memoriam reliquisti: tribue, quaesumus; ita nos corporis et sanguinis tui sacra mysteria venerari, ut redemptionis tuae fructum in nobis jugiter sentiamus."

* III, Q. lxxiii, Art. vi.

CHAPTER X

IN theological matters the spark that illumines always comes from under the hoof of strict reasoning. To conceive the sacrifice of Mass as a sacrament is a simple visualisation of a great truth which, if it be once grasped by the mind, even were it after a painful logical process, makes all the difference between light and phantasy. The great Christian sacrifice is essentially a sacramental mystery; this fact we have established to our satisfaction. Let us now see how such a conclusion affects the working of our faith. I am not yet giving the explanation of the way in which a sacrament can be a sacrifice; this will be our next task; just now I am interested in the mental attitude of one who knows clearly that the sacrifice of Mass is a sacramental thing. I want to speak of that liberty of mind possessed by the Catholic people, who may well be called, in the words of S Peter, " a royal priesthood," in their dealings with one of the most tremendous mysteries that has been proposed to man's acceptance. Believing the divine sacrifice of the Mass to be a sacrament, they are asked to envisage the fact that takes place on the altar in a way which creates a mentality absolutely apart from everything. They are asked to visualise mentally two things; first, that on the altar, at a given moment, easily timed, there is offered up the perfect sacrifice whose elements are absolutely divine, being, in fact, the Body and Blood of Christ. But they are asked also not to give to that sacrifice a meaning which is in any way a natural meaning, as if there were a sacrifice in the sense in which sacrifices have been offered here on earth by men, as if there were any of that element of destruction which has been the common property of all natural sacrifices. In other words, the principle that at Mass we have as sacrifice a sacrament implies two things, and it implies them equally immediately: firstly, that there is a real sacrifice; secondly, that it is a sacrifice such as has not been known to human experience.

It is of utmost importance, in order to safeguard the sacramentality of the sacrifice of Mass, to eliminate from it all such things as would make it into a natural sacrifice, a human act, with human sensations and human circumstances. It must be a thing in which the ordinary laws of nature have no part, otherwise it would be, not a sacrament, but a natural event. In order to remain orthodox it is just as necessary to preserve in our minds the sacramentality of the sacrifice of Mass as its reality in containing a divine victim. This aspect I call the negative aspect in the sacramental concept of the sacrifice of Mass.

We grant without further discussion that a sacrifice is the supreme mode of divine worship; we also hold it as certain that the Son of God, when dying on the cross, was a true sacrifice to God. This divine sacrifice, together with all the ritual sacrifices that preceded it and prefigured it under the old dispensation, we have to call natural sacrifices, as they exhibit features which are observed by our natural powers of knowledge. Death, which is the most universal element in sacrifice, is an easily observable thing; the death of Christ on the cross could be seen by all men: " They shall look on him whom they have pierced " is S John's last phrase in the narration of the passion. The natural sacrifice is essentially a thing of human observation and human experience. Now the Eucharistic sacrifice is the very opposite; no human experience will tell us the nature of that sacrifice; such a sacrifice is not meant to come under human experience. The sacrifice which is a sacrament belongs to an order of things which could never be known to us except through faith. It is called commonly the mystical sacrifice, or also the unbloody sacrifice; but there is no substitute for the one word which alone expresses the matter completely, that it is a sacrament which at the same time is sacrifice, or, better still, that the sacrifice is sacrament. The term " sacramental sacrifice " is no doubt the best term, though, for accuracy of language, I should prefer this simple verbal equation, the sacrament-sacrifice.

When, therefore, we meditate on our great sacrifice of the altar, we need not in the least think of any such scene as took place on Calvary; we need not think of the anguish of pain, of any laceration of body; we need not even think of any hypothetical death; in fact, all the things that constitute the natural sacrifice ought to be far removed from our thoughts. My reader will do me the service not to misunderstand me here. When assisting at Mass he may meditate on all the terrible and painful circumstances of Christ's historic passion and death; there could be no more appropriate subject of contemplation at such a time; what I mean is this, that none of those natural details of Christ's sacrificial act on the cross are to be read into the sacrament-sacrifice which takes place on the altar. The Catholic is exhorted over and over again to remember that he is assisting at an unbloody sacrifice; by this expression is meant much more than a mere absence of gruesome circumstance. The expression signifies a total diversity of the two sacrifices, one being *in natura*, the other being *in sacramento;* this is the greatest difference imaginable. Sacrifice *in sacramento* is not merely an attenuated, a mild form of the natural sacrifice; the two have nothing in common except the divine Thing that is being immolated. We Catholics have that great freedom of mind through our faith in the reality of the Eucharistic sacrifice; we know that through this faith we move in a world which is entirely beyond human experience; we are true mystics, because we hold an infinite reality and yet hold it without any human factors; it is truly the *mysterium fidei,* the mystery of the faith. We surround the celebration of the Eucharistic sacrifice with every kind of imitation of Christ's real sacrifice on the cross; we multiply the sign of the cross over the elements; Mass is a spiritual drama, a mystery play, of the finest order; we love to remember every one of the events that took place between the Garden of Olives and the sepulchre in which Christ's body was laid; but we know also that the sacrament which is being celebrated through it all, and under cover of it all, considered in itself, has no such human accidents; that it is a simple thing, without succession of events, and though it be in our hands, it is still worlds apart from the world in which we live.

The Catholic has never found it difficult to see the fitness of Christ's concluding words when he announced the mystery of his Flesh and his Blood to be eaten and drunk by man: " The words that I have spoken to you are spirit and life."* We find in this utterance the very thing that is dear to us: the profound difference between the natural order and the sacramental order.

It is a cherished theme for the Christian doctors to extol the spiritual, or better still, the immaterial character of the Eucharistic sacrament; and all through Christian literature there flows this double current, the one of faith in the reality of the divine Thing that is contained in the sacrament, and the other of delight in the absolute other-worldliness of

* John vi 64.

91

the sacrament. The sacramental sphere is an unknown world with a well-known inhabitant.

Could we doubt one moment the faith of S Thomas in the Real Presence ? Yet S Thomas is one of the most spiritual theologians in this matter of the Eucharist; he is far from being an ultra-realist. In this he resembles S Augustine more closely than any modern theologian. Passages like the following, taken from the *Summa*, have a strong Augustinian flavour; yet they never leave the solid ground of the sacramental reality: " In this sacrament (of the Eucharist) Christ himself is contained, not indeed in his own kind, but in the kind of the sacrament " (" In hoc sacramento continetur ipse Christus non quidem in specie propria, sed in specie sacramenti "). Therefore it is possible to eat Christ spiritually in a twofold manner; in one manner as he exists in his own kind, and in this way the angels eat spiritually Christ himself, in so far as they are united with him in the enjoyment of perfect charity and in the clear vision, which sort of bread we also expect to find in heaven, such union not being by faith only, as we have it here on earth. The other way of eating Christ spiritually is of Christ as he is under the appearances of the sacrament, in so far, namely, as a man believes in Christ with a desire of receiving the sacrament; and this is not only eating Christ spiritually, but also eating the sacrament itself, a thing that does not belong to the angels; and therefore, though it behoves the angels to eat Christ spiritually, it does not behove them to eat the sacrament spiritually."*

Let me just add, as a word of comment, that here S Thomas does not speak of spiritual communion, in the modern sense, but of the worthy sacramental communion which supposes faith and desire.

Another golden phrase is to be found in the same passage: " Sacraments are proportionate to faith, through which truth is seen through a glass in a dark manner, and therefore, speaking exactly, it behoves not angels, but men to eat the sacrament spiritually."

I have already exhorted my reader to rejoice in the truth that sacraments are signs, and not to give up any of the glory of sacramental symbolism because Protestantism has distorted the traditional notion of sacramental signification. In the same line of thought let me exhort him now to defend against all comers the spiritual character of our sacraments; although Protestantism again has made of this

* III, Q. lxxx, Art. ii.

notion of spirituality an emptying out of the contents of the sacrament. Though the text just cited from S Thomas refers more directly to the eating of the bread of the Eucharist, its spirit applies to the Eucharistic sacrifice as well. We are truly dealing with a spiritual sacrifice in the sense that there is no death in it, though there be in it all that reality which is indispensable to the sacrifice.

We know the theological grounds on which Protestantism first rejected the notion that in the Eucharist there was a sacrifice besides a partaking. If there were a sacrifice, it was objected, it would mean that Christ's sacrifice on the cross was not complete. The whole answer to this will be given by-and-by; but let us say it at once, is it not in the very nature of the sacrament-sacrifice not to supplement, or even to complement, the sacrifice in nature ? The two sacrifices belong to entirely different spheres or modes of being; one could never, to use a colloquial phrase, stand in the way of the other. Such errors could only arise in the minds of men who could not see what the sacrament really means; when once we admit that the sacrament-sacrifice has not a vestige of that which constitutes the natural sacrifice, *cadit quaestio.*

In the same order of thought it would be

flimsy theology, to say the least, to make the Eucharistic sacrifice in any way to be part of Christ's natural sacrifice; to say, for instance, that the Last Supper ought to be considered as the first act in Christ's passion and death; such a linking up with the natural sacrifice is again contrary to the very essence of the sacrament, which could never be an integral part of a natural proceeding. Christ's natural sacrifice and Christ's Eucharistic sacrifice stand to each other in a relationship which is truly wonderful, and of which there is no other instance in the whole realm of revealed truth; one represents the other, but one does not complete the other. The oneness of Christ's redemptive sacrifice is a matter of Catholic dogma; but this oneness is preserved then only if we make the great distinction of S Thomas, that on Calvary Christ was offered up *in propria specie* and that on the altar he is offered up *in specie sacramenti*. The oneness is truly saved through the total diversity of the two states.

The freedom of the Catholic mind is supreme; we are not bound by any sentiment or imagination; we know that Christ is offered on the altar, and our way of conceiving this fact, the greatest of all earthly facts, is more ethereal than the sunbeam. Let the spiritual thing be held spiritually by the spiritual man.

CHAPTER XI

THE SACRAMENTAL VIEW OF THE SACRIFICE OF THE MASS IN ITS POSITIVE ASPECT

IN the preceding chapter we have dropped those limitations with which man's imagination is always tempted to fetter the things of God. Imaginative presentments are not dangerous to faith provided we know their provisional character.

We come now to the real content of that sacrament whose mode of being is so far beyond all known qualifications. How is a sacrament a sacrifice? In answering this question we shall also answer the subsidiary question, How is the sacrament the food of the soul, as the Eucharistic food is essentially the banquet that follows the sacrifice? Here more than ever we must cling for our guidance to the all-important principle that we are truly dealing with a sacrament whose very essence it is to be a relationship of signification. We must approach the question of what is contained in the sacrament through the signs that constitute the sacrament, and not *vice versa*. It would be quite an erroneous proceeding to say first that the Body and Blood of Christ are contained in the sacrament, and to conclude from this to the sacrifice. Such is not the sacramental proceeding. Our method ought to be quite other. Let us take the signs, both as things and as words; examine these signs, and see whether they do really signify a sacrifice; if they do signify a sacrifice, then there is a sacrifice, according to the universal adage in this matter that the Christian sacraments do what they signify: *Sacramenta efficiunt quod significant.* This is an extremely important point of view, a real cross-roads in theological thinking. We know the hidden content of the sacrament through the external sign both in things and words, or, to be more technical, in matter and form. The whole power of significance comes back to us here. If God, in his omnipotence, without any human ministry, without any external symbolism, gave grace to the soul of the heathen, this would be an act of mercy, wonderful indeed, but entirely unsacramental. We know nothing about it; we have neither message nor revelation about it. When, on the other hand, a heathen is baptised by another human being, in the Name of the Father and of the Son and of the Holy Ghost, we know what happens in the heathen's soul, through that very clear and significant symbolism of the first sacrament. We read the state of the baptised man in the rite of Baptism; we do not read the significance of the rite through the state of his soul, which is not visible to us. Baptism in its traditional, sacramental form is for us the key that opens the understanding to the excellency of the Christian soul. So in this sacrament of the Eucharist, we know that it is a sacrifice because its words and its elements clearly signify sacrifice; we know that there is the Body and Blood of Christ because the sacrament signifies the Body and Blood of Christ as clearly as Baptism signifies the washing of the soul in the Father and the Son and the Holy Ghost. Everything else that makes the Eucharist such a marvel of divine power follows upon the signification, but does not precede it. Bread is changed into Christ's Body, wine is changed into Christ's Blood, because the sacramental signification absolutely exacts such a change: for if such a change did not take place the Eucharistic significance would be a false and lying thing.

This S Thomas expresses in a sentence which we ought to remember at every turn: "Verba, quibus fit consecratio, sacramentaliter operantur: unde vis conversiva, quae est in formis horum sacramentorum, consequitur significationem " (" The words through which the [Eucharistic] consecration takes place work sacramentally; therefore the power of changing, which is in the forms of these sacraments, follows upon the signification ").*

The meaning of this becomes more clear and also more informative when we consider that S Thomas makes a distinction here between the simple power of God and the sacramental power. God, in this sacrament as well as in the other sacraments, works not through simple omnipotence; he works sacramentally, because he makes the external signs to have full and complete internal truth and reality, which is a different thing from an absolute act of omnipotence.

Suppose, says S Thomas in so many words, that God said: " Let this be my Body " in an absolute way, without any historic significance of meaning, as God said at the beginning: " Let there be light "; such an act of God would have nothing in common with the Christian sacrament, because, as is evident, the all-important element of significance would be excluded from such a divine fiat. The Eucharistic sacrament is performed, not through a

* III, Q. lxxviii, Art. iv ad 3m

divine imperative, but through a divine symbolism, or, if you like better, through a divine remembrance of the past. This most interesting passage of S Thomas must be quoted in its entirety; more than anything I have read, it helps one to grasp the real nature of a sacrament.

To the objector who says that the best formula for Christ in the Eucharistic consecration would have been the imperative: " Let this be my body," as God had said: " Let light be " and light was, S Thomas replies: " To the second objection I answer that the same word of God that worked in the creation of things also works in this consecration; this, however, in one way in the one instance, and in another way in the other instance: for here (in the sacrament) it works effectively and sacramentally, that is to say, according to the power of signification, and therefore it is necessary that in this phrase the final result of the consecration should be signified by a substantive verb of the indicative mood and of the present tense. But in the creation of things it worked only effectively, which efficiency is indeed through the command of his wisdom; and therefore in the creation of things the divine word is expressed in a verb of the imperative mood, according to the first chapter of Genesis: ' Be light made, and light was made.' "*

These considerations are simply indispensable to any clear understanding of the Eucharistic mystery. God's omnipotence in the Eucharist, in the words of S Thomas, is sacramental because it carries out what it signifies in speech and thing—*i.e.*, in the external signification. God's omnipotence does not place directly, immediately, through an imperative fiat, the Body and Blood of Christ on the altar; but God—*i.e.*, the Son of God—at the Last Supper first, and through the priestly minister after, says things and performs rites which signify the sacrifice of his Body and of his Blood; and we conclude that there is in that sacramental act of signification the sacrifice of the Body and Blood of Christ, otherwise the divine signification would be a falsehood. But may I not say that we ought to be more intent on the things Christ does and says at the Last Supper than on a possible nature of the unseen thing; for had Christ put his Body and his Blood on the table at the Last Supper absolutely, without any concomitant historical element of representation and memory, the thing would have been some-

* III, Q. lxxviii, Art. ii ad 2m.

thing totally different from the Christian Eucharist.

It is certain that the Son of God could have given to his Church a definite rite, made up of actions and words, of symbols and expressions which would have been a most telling representation of his sacrifice on the cross, without such a rite having an inward kernel, so to speak, without its containing the thing it symbolised. The Christian Eucharist is such a rite, plus the inward kernel; it is a perfect rite, extremely significative; but it goes just one degree beyond mere signification, it contains what it signifies. Yet, let us say it over and over again, it contains no more than it signifies; for did it contain more than it signified it would not be a sacrament, but an absolute act of God's hidden omnipotence, an act about which we know nothing. It is perfectly futile in theology to ask questions about the nature of the Eucharistic sacrifice beyond that clearly-marked outline of significance. If in order to explain the nature of the Eucharistic sacrifice we had to fall back upon hidden realities of a divine nature not adumbrated by the external signification of the sacrament, we should not only leave the certain for the uncertain, but we should desert the sacramental plane entirely in quest of the unknown.

Let us approach the same subject, so tremendously vital in Catholic thought, from another angle.

Sometimes Catholic apologists of the Real Presence have said that bread and wine are the most unlikely symbols anyone could choose to stand for body and blood. The intention of such well-meaning writers is evident; they are up in arms against Protestant theology, which says that the Eucharist is an excellent symbol of Christ's Body and Christ's Blood, but a symbol only. In order to confute the Protestant theologian the simple-minded apologist flatly denies the significative power of the Eucharistic elements, and thinks that the words of Christ at the institution must mean the Real Presence because bread and wine could never, even with a strong stretch of imagination, be symbols of body and blood. But who does not see that such defenders deeply compromise Catholic theology? By all means let us protect Catholic doctrine, but *non talibus auxiliis*. Our good friends seem to rejoice in the downright arbitrariness of the divine fiats. We have said already that we Catholics must defend the sacramental sign with greater tenacity of purpose than anyone else. If the Eucharistic elements were not expressive and symbolic, what would become of the notion of sacrament? The sacrament must signify in words and deeds and things, shall we say, to the breaking-point, to the point where it will be necessary, if a lie is to be avoided, that the sacrament should contain what it signifies. It is as if a man succeeded in acting the part of a king on some mighty stage with such splendour, such wealth, such a number of retainers, such an equipment of military parade, that people would ask themselves the question, where is the difference between this actor-king and the real king? perhaps hereditary title would be the only thing missing. In the sacrament the Church must act the spiritual thing with such clearness, power, and directness that no one will question her meaning; she really means to accomplish what she acts, as it were, on the stage of sacramental symbolism. The inward thing of the sacrament is the prolongation of the signification of the sacrament. Having gone thus far in saying and doing sacramental things we cannot stop, we have evoked the divine ghost, and we cannot lay him. We all know of the blasphemous nomenclature of the more ignoble sort of Protestantism which applies the hideous word " incantation " to the simple sacramental faith of Catholicism. An incantation is a use of words and symbols so strong that the spirits are tied to them through the very vehemence of expression. I, for one, shall not blush for the accusation if, in my priestly office, I am supposed to use words and things so expressive that they must have the divine thing irrevocably tied unto them. I am not making arbitrary signs and pronouncing words of mere convention, when I officiate at the altar and when I consecrate at the sacring bell; I am performing a rite which, if seen in its whole setting, must mean the Body and Blood of Christ as a sweet odour of sacrifice.

Sacramental significance, then, is the only door through which we approach the nature of Christ's sacrifice on the altar. We possess what we signify, neither more nor less; if there is more, it is no longer the sacrament; if there is less, we are deceived. The whole question, then, is whether the Eucharistic rite—the words and deeds of Christ first, our words and our deeds, acting in the Person of Christ, secondarily—does signify Christ's death on the cross in its literal reality. The Catholic Church has always maintained that such is the case, and this is why she believes in the sacrifice of the Mass. This book is not against heretics, but it is for

Catholics; so I do not think it is my duty to defend the Catholic position here. My task is to explain to the believer the nature of the sacrifice of the Catholic altar, and the sacrifice is nothing else than the inward kernel of the external, symbolical rite of sacrifice.

The study of the Canon of the Mass is extremely instructive in the light of all that has been said in this chapter. Before and after the essentially sacramental act of consecration, which we may call the major rite of sacrifice, there are minor sacrificial rites and prayers surrounding the central act, making it more and more expressive, helping it in its work of signification, and leading up gradually from the human to the divine, emphasising that very thing which I have stated above when I said that the inward thing of the sacrament is the prolongation of the external signification of the sacrament.

Let us take the invocation that immediately precedes the solemn moment of consecration: " Quam oblationem tu, Deus, in omnibus, quaesumus, benedictam, adscriptam, ratam, rationabilem, acceptabilemque facere digneris: ut nobis Corpus et Sanguis fiat dilectissimi Filii tui Domini nostri Jesu Christi " (" This our offering, do thou, O God, vouchsafe in all things to bless, consecrate, approve, make reasonable and acceptable: that it may become for us the Body and Blood of thy most beloved Son, our Lord Jesus Christ ").

We need not give to the prayers of the Canon, with the exception of the consecration words, a higher origin than the Church's own inspirations; but they show clearly how the Church understood from the very beginning the great truth that the Eucharistic sacrifice is neither more nor less than the reality signified by the sacramental rite. The Church could, with such a faith, supplement the essential signification of the sacrament which is of divine institution with her own significations and symbolisms, which are like so many extensions and radiations of the divine sign. This the Church did for all the other sacraments; the rite of Baptism, for instance, from the very early period of Christianity, contained acts and symbols which are an evident addition to the baptismal regeneration as enunciated by Christ in the Gospels. The glorious rite of the Christian Mass, centring round the traditional action of the Last Supper, is the most potent instance of that profound instinct of the Catholic Church which tells her that the external sign is the measure and guarantee of the internal reality.

CHAPTER XII

THE ESSENCE OF THE EUCHARISTIC SACRIFICE

KEENNESS for divine things and love of objective truth have oftentimes led Catholic divines to the very threshold of the unknown. In this matter of the Eucharistic sacrifice they have tried to find out whether there is, or there is not, something that happens in Christ's own self so as to establish him in the state of Victim on our altars. The more extreme spirits among them have looked for the essence of the Eucharistic sacrifice in Christ's own self, not in the sacrament. Their sense of reality seems to remain unsatisfied until Christ's own self be directly touched by the knife of immolation. In their controversy with the Protestant symbolists they have become extreme realists, perhaps ultra-realists, and they end by explaining the sacrifice of Mass in terms of Person, no longer in terms of sacrament. It is as if they conceived the *processus* of the Eucharistic sacrifice to be something in the following order. The glorious Person of Christ is produced on the altar through the power of consecration; under the sacramental veil, no doubt, yet directly in its totality; and, once produced, it is immolated and offered up as the perfect sacrifice, in some mysterious, indefinable manner. They would call it, perhaps, sacramental manner, though by an abuse of words, but their commonest term is the word " mystical." In other words, they put Christ's self first, the sacrifice and the sacrament after. This is, I think, a fair description of much theological and devotional phraseology inside the liberal tolerance of Catholic dogma.

At first sight it may seem an easier, and even more helpful, concept of the Eucharistic sacrifice, to think of Christ's glorious Person as being in a mysterious way on the altar, as dying mystically, and as being offered up mystically; yet when we come to strict theology, and when we have to state the Eucharist in terms which will make it possible for us to defend it against all enemies, we can no longer express the nature of the Catholic sacrifice in the way just indicated. Shall we say that no one need be disturbed if, for the practical working of his devotion, he adopts the *processus* of thought I have described ? The contents of the Eucharistic mystery are so great that whosoever holds faithfully to Transubstantiation and the Real

Presence cannot err substantially ever after. At the same time there is a need for clear thinking in this sublime matter as in everything else, if sentiment, even pious sentiment, is to be kept within the bounds of the objective realities.

It is evident that S Thomas, who represents so much of Catholic thought and tradition, is far from that view of the Eucharistic sacrifice which I have given above. At no time does S Thomas feel the need of asking himself whether anything wonderful happens within Christ's own self when Mass is offered up; in fact, it is a cardinal point of his theology to deny every kind of change in Christ's own Person in the whole Eucharistic *processus*. S Thomas is too keen and too clear-headed a sacramentalist ever to become an ultra-realist; even when he says that Christ is immolated in the sacrament, his whole mode of thinking is sacramental, as his words imply, not natural, in the sense in which in a former chapter we opposed the sacrament to nature.

A long study of the Eucharistic doctrine of S Thomas fills one with admiration for his power of grasping a truth and never swerving from it. When one sees how constant has been the tendency of pious men to slip from sacramental thought into natural thought one cannot help admiring S Thomas, who does not show one single instance of such a lapse.

The essence, then, of the sacrifice of Mass ought to be completely stated before we reach Christ in the personal aspect; that is to say, the Eucharistic sacrifice is not directly a mystery of Christ's Person, but it is directly a mystery of Christ's Body and Blood. Christ's Body is offered up, Christ's Blood is offered up; these are the inward kernel of the external sign in the sacrificial rite; and beyond these—the Body and the Blood—the sacrament, as sacrament, does not go. No conclusion could be more certain. If the Eucharist is to remain a sacrament in our theology, the Body of Christ and the Blood of Christ must be that divine prolongation of our sacramental *actio* at Mass, otherwise the sacrament would not signify the truth. Body and Blood must be the inward kernel of the external signification. In this we must find the whole essence of the sacrifice; I might almost say we must rest content with this and not go beyond, as we have no authority to go beyond.

When we offer up the great sacrifice we say that we are acting Christ's death sacramentally. Now, Christ's death is Body and Blood separated; we do neither more nor less when we sacrifice at the altar. We do not enter directly into the mystery of Christ's Person; we enter into the mystery of Christ's Body and Blood. In the mystery of Christ's Body and Blood we must find the essence of the Eucharistic sacrifice.

The sacrifice of Mass, then, is this, that we have a separation between Christ's Body and Christ's Blood brought about, not by a fiat of God's omnipotence, irrespective of any precedent or human connections, but as a prolongation, as the inward kernel of reality, of the whole commemorative rite which historically, and as an unbroken chain of remembrance, is linked up with the dead Christ on the cross. Separation of Body and Blood on the altar in itself, absolutely considered, would not make a sacrifice; nor would a figurative rite make a true sacrifice; but the two together, one as the human act of commemoration, and the other as the divine prolongation, the infinitely real inwardness, of that same act, make the Eucharistic sacrifice. Were we to admit that in the sacrifice of Mass there is some mysterious change in the state of Christ's self, this change could not be anywhere else than in his Body and in his Blood, as the words of consecration do not signify anything sacramentally beyond Body and Blood. Suppose, for the sake of argument, that the immolation of Christ on the altar really affected the Person of Christ, it could not affect him except in his Body and in his Blood. It is the Body that is offered up, it is the Blood that is poured out in virtue of the consecration words. By all the laws of sacramental reality we ought not to look for the essence of the sacrifice to any other portions of Christ than his Body and his Blood, supposing even that an internal change in Christ were necessary in order to make Mass a real and actual sacrifice. But S Thomas has succeeded in giving to Mass the highest degree of sacrificial reality, nay, even of immolation, without the necessity of any change whatever in Christ's own self.

It is the misfortune of anyone who undertakes to expound these high matters that he has constantly to promise further explanations, as he feels, as by instinct, the reader's temporary bewilderment. Here I have to promise a chapter to be written on the nature of Eucharistic concomitance, where it will be shown how the whole Person of Christ, with all the adjuncts of a complete life, may be in the Eucharist, though the concept of the Eucharistic sacrifice discards everything except the Body and Blood of Christ.

The Council of Trent insists emphatically on the distinction of role between sacrament and concomitance, copying, almost word for word, the language of S Thomas himself. But it is no exaggeration to say that for the purpose of explaining the sacrifice of Mass we need not remember anything else except Christ's Body and Christ's Blood. To such an extent is this accurate that if Mass had been celebrated by one of the Apostles directly after Christ's death on the cross, when Body and Blood were separated, and Christ's Soul was in limbo, there would have been as complete and as true a sacrifice as on any Christian altar to-day. The principal portion of Christ's Person, his Soul, would not have been united to that Body and that Blood; but this could make no difference in the sacramental sacrifice as the sacramental signification terminates directly and exclusively in Christ's Body and Christ's Blood.

This hypothesis is made much of by S Thomas and the other medieval theologians. " The soul of Christ is in the sacrament through real concomitance, because it is not without the body; but it is not in the sacrament through the power of consecration, and therefore if this sacrament had been consecrated or celebrated at the time when the soul was really separated from the body, the soul of Christ would not have been under the sacrament."* And again: " If at the time of Christ's passion when the blood was really separated from the body of Christ this sacrament had been consecrated, under the appearance of bread there would only have been the body, and under the appearance of wine there would only have been the blood."†

It is evident from the very nature of the hypothesis here made by S Thomas that the reality of the Eucharistic sacrifice could never depend on an intrinsic change, either in Christ's Person or in Christ's Body and Blood at the moment of the sacrificial immolation on the Christian altar. May we not say that the Eucharistic immolation by its very nature is supposed to take Christ's Body and Christ's Blood such as it finds them, in the state in which they happen to be ? The immolation itself never causes a new state, either in Christ's Person or in Christ's Body and Blood. If Christ, considered in his natural existence, be a mortal man like ourselves, as he was at the Last Supper, the Eucharistic immolation is accomplished in the mortal Body and Blood; if Christ, in his natural existence, be in the

* III, Q. lxxxi, Art. iv ad 3m.
† III, Q. lxxxi, Art. iv ad 2m.

glorious state as he is now in heaven, the Eucharistic immolation is accomplished in an immortal Body and Blood; if Christ be really dead, the Eucharistic immolation is accomplished in a Body and Blood which are not inhabited by the Soul which gives life. In other words, the Eucharistic immolation is above the states either of Christ's Person or of Christ's Body and Blood; it does not cause any state. Such varieties of state are caused by Christ's natural mode of existence at the time. This projection, as we might call it, of either the passing or the permanent state of Christ, as considered in his natural existence, into the Eucharistic existence is thus stated by S Thomas: " Whatever belongs to Christ as considered in himself (*i.e.*, what is intrinsic to Christ) may be attributed to him both in his natural existence and in his sacramental existence, such as to live, to die, to suffer pain, to be animate or inanimate, and other such attributes. But whatever concerns Christ in connection with external bodies (*i.e.*, what is extrinsic to Christ), can be attributed to him in his natural existence only, and not in his sacramental existence, such as to be mocked, to be spat upon, to be crucified, to be scourged, and other such things."*

* III, Q. lxxxi, Art. iv.

The meaning of S Thomas is clear and extremely important. Variety of state in the sacrament only comes from variety of state in Christ's natural existence; sacramental immolation, as such, does not cause a new variety of state. As a further and even bolder hypothesis S Thomas takes it for granted that if an Apostle had consecrated actually at the moment of Christ's dying, or if the consecrated elements had been preserved during the whole drama of Christ's agony on the cross, there would have been real suffering and real death in the blessed sacrament then, though there would not have been in the sacrament the external violence done to Christ's Body by the executioners. This S Thomas expresses thus: " And therefore Christ as he is under the sacrament cannot suffer (*i.e.*, external violence), but he can die " (" Et ideo Christus, secundum quod est sub hoc sacramento, pati non potest, potest tamen mori ").* This, of course, refers to the hypothetical sacramental presence at the moment of the crucifixion.

Suppositions like this are very instructive because they bring home to us the great truth that if there are changes in Christ's state under the Eucharistic form, such changes are not the

* III, Q. lxxxi, Art. iv ad 1m.

result of the sacramental immolation, but they are anterior to it; we offer up at the altar the Body and Blood such as we find them, I say this again.

It may be described as a tendency of modern piety to read into the mystery of the Eucharistic sacrifice certain elements of a more drastic kind which seem to give greater reality to the Eucharistic immolation than is warranted by the strictly sacramental view. But let us remember over and over again that in the sacrament we are not dealing with the natural life of Christ; we are dealing with his representative life, representing the natural life. The Eucharistic Body and the Eucharistic Blood represent Christ's natural Body and Christ's natural Blood. The Protestant would go so far as to say that the Eucharistic bread and wine represent Christ's Body and Christ's Blood; the Catholic goes beyond that and says that Christ's Eucharistic Body under the appearance of bread, and Christ's Eucharistic Blood under the appearance of wine, represent Christ's natural Body and Christ's natural Blood as they were on Calvary. This is the true and final expression of sacramental representation; and such representation suffices by itself to constitute the sacrifice, because the representation is of that period of Christ's wonderful existence when he was nothing but sacrifice, as his Blood was separated from his Body.

Protestantism has denied the Eucharistic sacrifice on various grounds, into which we need not enter for the moment. The non-Catholic attitude which in a way is nearest to Catholicism is that frame of mind which admits all, or nearly all, of the Catholic doctrine of the Real Presence, and yet denies the Eucharistic sacrifice. It is a belief in the Eucharist minus the sacrifice. The earlier periods of Protestantism, chiefly of Lutheranism, exhibited that attitude of an almost total faith in the Eucharistic realities combined with fierce denial of the Eucharistic sacrifice.

To meet this kind of unbelief the Church might have adopted two modes of defence; she might have said that the whole Eucharistic doctrine, as it stands, as the Scriptures reveal it, as those very Protestants of the meeker type hold it, with the dual consecration, must be a sacrifice if it has any meaning at all; that the Church, in her Eucharistic liturgy as handed down from the Apostles, is a sacrificant as well as a communicant, from the very nature of the case.

Or the Church might have appealed to

another revelation, as if she had said that she knew through tradition that the Eucharistic rite contained a hidden element of sacrifice which is not evident in the rite itself, but which is known to the Church in virtue of her revelation *ad hoc*. The Church then would have made it her principal business to produce the authentic proofs of such revelation.

It is evident that the line of defence of the Church has been the former of the two alternatives. The Church has maintained that the Eucharistic rite, as she learned it from Christ and his Apostles, with the dual consecration and all the sacramental signification that surrounds it, is a true sacrifice. The Church does not appeal to a hidden element, to something recondite, not manifested in Eucharistic revelation such as it stands in the Scriptures. The Church says this: the Eucharist as we have learned it from the Son of God and his Apostles, as even those well-meaning Protestants hold it, is an evident sacrifice in the eyes of all those who have the clear vision of the things of Christ.

CHAPTER XIII

EUCHARISTIC REPRESENTATION, APPLICATION, IMMOLATION

IN the Eucharistic mystery Body and Blood exist separately — through a sacramental separation completely sufficient for the purpose—though the natural Person of Christ be whole and entire.

Christ, who gave his Body and Blood to the Apostles at the Last Supper, was whole and entire at the head of the festive board. The Christ whose Body and Blood is on the Catholic altar is whole and entire in heaven. Now the Body and Blood of the Eucharist are representations of the Christ in the state in which he was not whole and entire, but when he was broken up into parts on the cross at his death. The Eucharistic Body and the Eucharistic Blood, therefore, at the Last Supper, were the representation, or, to choose our word more accurately, the presentation, of the Christ who would be broken up the day after, not of the Christ who was there at the head of the table. The Eucharistic Body and the Eucharistic

Blood on our altars are the representation—here the word (taken by its roots) is quite accurate—not of the Christ who is in heaven, but again of the Christ who was broken up on Calvary.

If we were to say that at the sacrifice of Mass Christ comes down from heaven and is sacrificed again, we should be expressing the mystery of the Eucharist in a totally wrong way. Such phrases, of course, may be allowed in ordinary devotional language; but they would be extremely inaccurate in strict theology. If by some supposition Christ came down from heaven in Person, however disguised, and if he were sacrificed on the altar, such an event, if at all possible, would be something quite different from the Eucharistic sacrifice. It is the very nature of the Eucharistic sacrifice to be a representation of the past, not a mactation in the present. Christ's Body and Blood represent aptly and completely that phase of Christ when he was dead on the cross; they do not represent in any way that other phase of Christ's existence, his glorious life in heaven. The full Person of Christ brought down on our altars could never be a representation of himself. The memory of the death of the Lord could never be the living Lord, but his Body and Blood, separated in sacramental truth, can be the memory or representation of that Lord whose Body was on the cross, whose Blood was poured out on the hill of Calvary.

The Eucharistic sacrifice, then, is essentially representative; it puts on the altar the Christ of Calvary, the great spectacle which Mary beheld as she gazed at the Body of her dead Son.

We have said already that every one of the seven sacraments is representative of the passion of Christ in its own way; but the Eucharist represents in a supremely realistic fashion, because it is what Christ was at one time, Body and Blood. When Christ was Body and Blood only he was the perfect sacrifice; and the Eucharist is perfect sacrifice because it is that literal rendering present—such is the true meaning of representation—of what there was on this earth of Christ after the *consummatum est* had been pronounced by him, when his Soul had been given up to the Father.

We have, therefore, in the Eucharist two degrees of signification which are interdependent and completive of each other. To have this additional degree of signification and representation of Christ's death makes the Eucharist the supreme sacrament, the king amongst sacraments. Let us remember what we have said of the distinction between 'sacrament' on the one hand, and 'sacrament and thing' on the other hand. In the Eucharist the 'sacrament and thing' are the Body and the Blood of Christ. Not only does the Eucharist have the power of signification as sacrament, but the Eucharist has the power of signification as 'sacrament and thing'; because the Body and the Blood of Christ in the Eucharist are representative—*i.e.*, as significative in extreme literalness of reality of the Christ on the cross.

Though we insist so much on the truth that at the consecration at the Catholic altar we come into contact directly, in virtue of the sacrament, with Christ's Body and Blood, not with his whole Person, the representation, which is the very nature of the Eucharistic sacrifice, terminates in the Person of Christ, but the broken Person of Calvary, not the whole Person of the Last Supper or of heaven.

That Christ should have ever been one who was Body and Blood in a state of separation gives to the Eucharistic separation of Body and Blood its whole meaning. The Eucharistic separation of Body and Blood is the memory, the representation of that real separation in historic time. Body and Blood separated would have no meaning but for the historic precedent in Christ's career when the last drop of his Blood left his Body. The Eucharistic representation is, indeed, a thing in which metaphors have no place; it is a thing of absolute literalness.

By application, we mean that individual benefit of every believer in Christ's passion; the merit, the sacrificial atonement of that great immolation on the cross comes down on the individual man and enters his soul. The Eucharistic sacrifice is the divine means for the individual believer to come into contact with the sacrifice of the cross; this is what we mean by application.

Here, again, I must be allowed to make a promise to my reader of a more ample treatment of the matter later on. At present I am concerned with the relationship of the Eucharistic Body and Blood with the Christ on the cross. As the Eucharistic Body and Blood are such a complete representation of the broken Son of God on Calvary, they are also the most immediate and complete contact of the soul with all the saving power of Golgotha. So it can be said that in the Eucharistic sacrifice Christ is truly immolated, because the immolation of Christ on Calvary is brought home to us in such a realistic manner. At Mass we do not say that Christ is immolated anew in the Eucharistic sacrifice, for this would mean a substantial process of disintegration in the very Person of Christ such as he is now, a thing not to be admitted. But we say that he is immolated, because the Calvary immolation is represented so truly, and is applied so directly, through the Eucharistic Body and Blood. It would not be enough, in order to explain the total range of the Eucharistic sacrifice, to say that at the altar we offer up the Body and Blood of Christ; we do more—we immolate the Christ, but not—and here is an immense difference—the Christ who is in heaven, because as such he is not represented on the altar at all, but the Christ of Calvary, as the Christ of Calvary is the only one who is represented on the altar.

It is, indeed, the one great thought that illumines the Eucharistic doctrine with a light as clear as the light of the rising sun that one phase of the divine career of the Son of God on earth is kept perpetually present amongst us with an exactness of repetition that is truly overwhelming when we come to meditate on it. After his death, and before the Resurrection, Christ was truly on this earth; but in what a state ! His Body was lifeless and bloodless, his Blood was poured out, and the earth drank it as it had drunk the blood of Abel; yet in this broken condition the Person of Christ remained, for the death of Christ was not as the death of Abel. Hypostatic union survived that great breaking up—that is to say, the divine Person of the Word remained united as before, both with the Body and the Blood of Christ; the Person of Christ as Person remained entire, though the human nature of Christ had been broken up; so that it may be said in all exactness of theological language, that the Body and the Blood on Calvary or in the sepulchre were Christ, on account of the divine Person hypostatically united. The Son of God never ceased to be a complete Person, even in death, a thing which is not to be admitted of the human dead, who cease to be persons in the real sense of the word.

This aspect of the Incarnation is so important and of such relevance to the Eucharistic mystery that I do not hesitate to enter into it more fully and to quote from an earlier portion of the Third Part of the *Summa*, where S Thomas treats of Christ's descent into limbo.

Question lii, Article iii runs thus: " Whether the whole Christ was in Limbo " (" Utrum Christus fuerit totus in inferno "). Quoting, to begin with, from S Augustine, the answer of S Thomas is in the affirmative. The Augustinian text runs thus: " The whole Son is with the Father; he is whole in heaven, whole on earth, whole in the womb of the Virgin, whole on the cross, whole in Hades, whole in Paradise, whither he ushered in the thief." And his own answer is as follows: " Though in death the soul of Christ was separated from the body, neither the soul nor the body were separated from the person of the Son of God . . . therefore in that triduum of the death of Christ we must confess that the whole Christ was in the sepulchre, because the whole person was there as having that body united to itself; and likewise the whole Christ was in Limbo, because the whole person of Christ was there by reason of the soul united to itself; moreover, the whole Christ was then everywhere by reason of the divine nature " (" In illo triduo mortis Christi dicendum est, quod totus Christus fuit in sepulchro: quia tota persona fuit ibi per corpus sibi unitum: et similiter totus fuit in inferno: quia tota persona Christi fuit ibi ratione animae sibi unitae: totus etiam Christus tunc erat ubique ratione divinae naturae ").*

Let us cull two precious sentences from the answers to the objectors. " The fact that the body of Christ was not in Limbo does not

* III, Q. lii, Art. iii

exclude the fact of the whole Christ being in Limbo; but it only means this, that in Limbo there was not the whole of that which belongs to the human nature."* " Through the oneness of soul and body the totality of the human nature is constituted, but not the totality of the divine person; and therefore after the separation of soul and body through death the whole Christ remained, but the human nature did not remain in its wholeness."†

Let us be quite assured that nothing is more orthodox than to speak of the dead Christ in the full amplitude of complete Personality.

We may, then, consider Christ's Person in three stages: his mortality, from the moment of his birth to the death on the cross; his immortality, from the Resurrection *in saecula saeculorum;* his death, a phase which lasted but a short time, yet which, in spite of that great severance between Body and Soul, between Flesh and Blood, is one of the three periods under which the Person of Christ is known to our faith. I do not crave my reader's forgiveness for bringing into play here some of the principles of the Hypostatic union. Could we ever expect to understand the Eucharist without its ramifications into the larger and profounder

* III, Q. lii, Art. iii ad 1m.   † *Ibid.*, ad 2m.

mystery of the union between a divine Person and the human nature? But who does not see how the Eucharist becomes a thing of palpitating reality if it is made clear that the one phase of the Christ-career which is the most sublime and the most heroic—his state of immolation as the divine Victim—is brought back to us in the identical elements that constituted it nearly two thousand years ago: Body on the one hand and Blood on the other hand, hypostatically united with the divine Person?

This, then, and nothing less, is meant by that representation which holds such a place in the traditional Eucharistic doctrine; this, and nothing less, is implied by that application to the individual soul of Christ's death on Calvary. All the treasures of Calvary, Body and Blood, clothed in divine Personality, are poured into our bosom; this, and nothing less, is the meaning of that immolation of Christ which Catholic tradition maintains as belonging to the Eucharistic sacrifice.

If the dead Christ on Calvary is a Victim that is immolated, then, of course, by sheer truth of equation, Christ is immolated on our altar, because that kind of Christ, that Christ of the second phase who was on Calvary, is on the altar in absolute identity. We do not think of the Christ of the first phase nor of the Christ of the third phase when we speak of the immolated Christ; we think of the Christ of the middle phase.

It is truly the *Christus passus* of S Thomas who is thus contained in the Eucharist. In virtue of the sacrament, the Eucharist contains, not the mortal Christ, nor even the dying Christ; nor does it contain the glorious Christ; but it contains the Christ directly after his death, though without any of the gaping wounds. " For as often as you shall eat this bread and drink the chalice, you shall shew the death of the Lord, until he come."*

From this we see that a very important distinction is necessary when we speak of Christ as being contained in the Eucharist. At the Last Supper, when the mortal Christ celebrated the Eucharistic mystery, in virtue of his direct act he was contained in the Eucharist in the same phase of his existence which was to come about soon after on Calvary; but in virtue of the concomitance he was contained in the fulness of the mortal phase of his divine Personality. If Mass had been celebrated during the three days of Christ's death the Eucharist would have contained the second

* 1 Cor. xi 26.

phase of the Christ-personality, and nothing more; there would have been no other concomitant personal quality. To-day on our altar, again in virtue of the sacrament, we have that second or middle phase of the Christ-personality; but in virtue of concomitance we have also the whole third phase in the Christ-personality, the glorious phase. But when treating of the sacrifice we need not think of any other rendering present except that of the second phase of the Christ-personality.

Such, then, is the content of the Eucharistic sacrament. Christ in the state of Victim before God, when his Body and Blood were unto the Lord a thing of sweet savour. " This is the difference between the Eucharist and the other sacraments which have an external matter, that the Eucharist contains a sacred thing absolutely, that is to say, Christ himself " (" Haec autem est differentia inter Eucharistiam et alia sacramenta habentia materiam sensibilem, quod Eucharistia continet aliquid sacrum absolute, scilicet ipsum Christum ").* " The Eucharist is the sacrament of the passion of Christ, inasmuch as man is rendered perfect by being linked up with the dead Christ " (" Eucharistia est sacramentum passionis Christi,

* III, Q. lxxiii, Art. i ad 3m.

prout homo perficitur in unione ad Christum passum ").*

Here again let me make use of the privilege of one who writes a stiff book to refer the reader to a later chapter, where we shall enter more fully into the nature of the sacrifice of the cross, and where it will be shown more clearly how Christ's sacrifice on the cross was essentially a thing of Body and Blood. But it is my fond conviction that I have made it clear in this chapter how we may, on the one hand, make of the sacramental Body and Blood of Christ the basis of all our thinking, and how, on the other hand, we come, through those divine elements, into direct and sacramental contact with the Person of Christ, I mean with the *Christus passus* of Calvary, who is the one represented, applied, immolated, and contained in the Eucharistic sacrifice.

* III, Q. lxxiii, Art. iii ad 3m.

CHAPTER XIV

THE ONENESS OF THE CHRISTIAN SACRIFICE

IT is well known that the most constant reproach of Protestantism against the Catholic doctrine of the Eucharistic sacrifice is this, that the Catholic Church, by teaching the need of a second sacrifice, virtually denies the all-sufficiency of the sacrifice on Calvary. But, on the other hand, through all her voices the Church has never ceased protesting that her Eucharistic sacrifice is by no means a derogation of the natural sacrifice of Christ on the cross, but that it is, on the contrary, an additional honour to that great act by which Christ redeemed us. The sacrifice of the Christian altar and the sacrifice of Calvary are one and the same sacrifice, says the Catholic Church. At the same time the Church maintains her faith that the Eucharistic sacrifice is a sacrifice in the true sense of the word, an act which is new every day, though the sacrifice be not new. We have, therefore, in this divine matter unity and duality of a very peculiar nature. It is my conviction that unless we cling firmly to the sacramental concept of the Eucharistic sacrifice we cannot meet the Protestant difficulty. But if once we grasp the meaning of the sacrament, the Protestant difficulty vanishes, and the fundamental oneness of the Christian sacrifice becomes apparent.

If the Eucharistic sacrifice were in any way a natural sacrifice it would be simply impossible to avoid the conclusion that there are two different sacrifices, and the query: Why two sacrifices ? would be most justifiable. The circumstance that the second sacrifice would take place under entirely different conditions would not save us from such a conclusion; if it be a sacrifice *in natura*, however it be disguised, it is truly another sacrifice, and, not the same sacrifice. But let the sacrifice be sacrament in the full sense of the word, it cannot be a new sacrifice, but it must be the representation, pure and simple, of the historic or natural sacrifice. If there were in the Eucharistic sacrifice an immolation, or a mactation, or a death, or an heroic deed, not contained already in the sacrifice of the cross, all at once the Eucharist would become sacrifice number two, because in such a supposition something new has happened in the world of grace which did not happen on the cross.

It is the genius of the Christian sacrament and also its very nature that it is an act which may be repeated indefinitely, though the content, or, if you like, the object of the act, be immutable.

This is the representative role of the Christian sacrament. Such a thing cannot happen anywhere outside the sacramental sphere. Is not the sacrament precisely this mystery of never ceasing repetition or representation of the thing that is immutable in itself ? If Christ came to us in his natural state and were offered up in his natural state, this new coming and this new offering would, indeed, be historic events which would form new chapters in the career of the Son of God. The sacramental presence and the sacramental offering are not historic events in the career of Christ; they do not form new chapters in the book of his life, though, of course, the act by which he instituted the Eucharist and offered up himself the first time are most tremendous deeds in his historic career, but to be offered up in the sacrament does not belong to the historic life of the Son of God. If there is repetition of acts, those repetitions are not on the part of Christ, they are on the part of the Church living here on earth. " As the thing which is offered up everywhere is one body and not many bodies, so there is one sacrifice everywhere " (" Sicut enim quod ubique offertur, unum est corpus, et non multa corpora, ita et unum sacrificium ").*

It is strange to see how an initial misconception in these high matters leads to profound divergences of thought, nay, even to dangerous presentments of Catholic truth. To save the oneness of the Christian sacrifice the strange hypothesis has been put forward in our own days that the Eucharistic sacrifice is not so much a representation of the sacrifice of the cross as an integral portion of the sacrifice of the cross. The Eucharistic sacrifices, both at the Last Supper and now, are being considered as so many stages in the one great all-embracing sacrifice whose culminating act was on the cross.

It is not my mission here to criticise theological opinions. It is certain, however, that to consider the Eucharistic sacrifice as being in any way a portion of the universal sacrifice is a profound reversal of the traditional role of the sacrament. A sacrament is not part of the drama, however great that drama may be; a sacrament is essentially the representation of the completed drama. The historic drama must be

* III, Q. lxxxiii, Art. i ad 1m.

complete before sacraments are possible. Sacraments are the monuments of the finished thing only, not the introductory scenes or the last acts of some great historic deed. If the Eucharistic sacrifice were in any way a portion of the universal sacrifice it would represent nothing except itself; it would contain nothing except itself; it would not apply to us anything except such grace as would belong to it in its partial role; it would not contain more immolation than would be warranted by its essentially limited place in a greater thing. Now the Christian sacrament, and above all, the sacrament-sacrifice, is a representation, an application, an immolation, and a containing of the whole immensity of the universal sacrifice. We must, if we are to save the dignity of the Catholic Mass, make it a thing by itself, not merely the first or last act of another thing, however divine and powerful.

I can understand the mental temptation that comes to anyone who lets go his grasp of the sacramental view in general, and more particularly of the sacramental view of the Eucharistic sacrifice. He finds himself confronted with an awkward duality, which he hopes to overcome by making Mass a part of the Christian sacrifice. He thus makes what might be called a oneness of organism, as if we were to call ' one ' the various members of the same body. In the theory I allude to, Mass is only a member, it is not the whole thing. But in the traditional view Mass is the whole thing; it contains the whole Christ with the kind of totality described in the last chapter. Is not one of the basic principles of the Eucharistic sacrifice to be found in the very completeness and finality of the sacrifice of the cross? If Mass gave anything to the cross it would cease to be a sacrament, as it would cease to be a representation. Mass is the memory or the monument of Christ's passion. Is it not the very purpose of a monument to stand for the complete victory, the heroic deed, the final triumph? We do not erect monuments to failures or things half-achieved. To take away something from the completeness of the sacrifice of the cross on the one hand, and on the other hand from the completeness of the sacrifice of the Mass, is not to join them into one organism, but it is to destroy them both. In this matter you cannot make a whole with two halves, because sacrament and nature are totally different. They become one through that very difference, as I have already said, because the one is the total representation of the other's totality of reality. The traditional view of the Church, as I shall prove by-and-by, is that the sacrifice of Calvary was complete and perfect in the genus sacrifice; the Eucharist adds nothing to it; but it is truly " the brightness of its glory and the figure of its substance."

To come back to the Protestant, we may say to him that his position is in a way comprehensible if he denies the whole sacramental system, root and branch, making of faith alone his approach to Christ; but if a man admits sacraments at all there is no more reason for him to reject the sacrament-sacrifice than to reject the sacrament-regeneration—*i.e.*, Baptism. In both we have nothing else than a representation—in the technical sense of the word—of Christ's death and its application to the individual soul. If Baptism is no derogation to Christ's sacrifice on Calvary, but is, on the contrary, the sign of Christ's victory, why should the Eucharistic sacrifice be such a derogation ? Are we not dealing in both instances with modes of contact between the individual soul and the historic Christ ? The Eucharistic sacrifice may be a more vivid contact, or, if you like, a more burning contact, having more of activity than of passivity, containing a divine substance; but when all is said, there is no radical difference in strict theological thought between Baptism and the Eucharist, considered in its true sacramental function of sacrifice and spiritual nutriment.

This is the place for the solution of a difficulty which may bewilder sometimes even careful thinkers in theological matters.

The Eucharistic sacrifice was offered up first at the Last Supper, before the natural sacrifice on the cross took place. Would not this point to the conclusion that in some way the Eucharistic sacrifice is truly the beginning of the whole sacrificial *processus* of Christ ? Did he not, when he offered himself in sacrifice in the supper room, perform the first act of that priesthood which reached consummation on Calvary ? Here, again, I admit that it would be difficult, not to say impossible, to fit the Last Supper into the act of redemption if we gave to the Eucharistic sacrifice the meaning and the value of a natural sacrifice. If it were a natural sacrifice, we could not avoid the conclusion that the world was redeemed before Christ shed his first drop of Blood, as the Last Supper would have had infinite value as sacrifice in its own right.

The other alternative would be, of course, the one adopted by some recent theologians whose views have already been mentioned, who consider the Last Supper to have been merely the first act of the one universal sacrifice, and who make the sacramental reality and the natural reality help each other. But if once the sacramental view of the Eucharistic sacrifice is admitted, the difficulty no longer exists. As the sacrament is essentially a representation, it could be instituted at any moment by Christ, provided he existed bodily in the reality of the Incarnation, and not only in the hope of the believer.

That great thing, the Christ immolated on the cross, could be represented before, as well as after, the cross, and though the sacrament derives all its worth and truth from the death of Christ, its institution, or even its celebration or use, may precede that death. The celebration of the Eucharistic sacrifice by Christ no more superseded the role of the cross than did the first breaking of bread of the Christian Church after the coming of the Holy Ghost. Sacraments, and sacraments only, possess that aloofness from the historical sequence of events.

Speaking of Baptism, S Thomas gives us in a very succinct fashion the theology of those wonderful anticipations by Christ. Taking it for granted that men may have received Chris-

tian Baptism before Christ died on the cross, he
says: " Even before Christ's passion Baptism
received its efficacy from Christ's passion, as it
was its figure; but it figured differently from
the sacraments of the old law, as these were
figures exclusively, but Baptism (before Christ's
death) was receiving the power of justifying
from that very Christ by whose virtue the
passion itself was to become the saving power "
(" Etiam ante passionem Christi baptismus
habebat efficaciam a Christi passione, inquantum eam praefigurabat: aliter tamen, quam
sacramenta veteris legis, nam illa erant figurae
tantum; baptismus autem ab ipso Christo
virtutem habebat justificandi, per cujus virtutem ipsa etiam passio salutifera fuit ").*

Applying this doctrine to the Eucharistic
sacrifice of the Last Supper, we may say that it
prefigured the sacrifice of the cross; and the
Christ who was to give his own natural Flesh
and Blood that power of redeeming mankind,
gave to bread and wine the power of representing sacramentally that same Flesh and
Blood. We need not even consider the Eucharistic sacrifice of the Last Supper as being a final
vow of the Son of God to undergo death, a
theme beloved of more than one preacher. The

* III, Q. lxvi, Art. ii ad 1m.

traditional view of the Last Supper is much more sacramental in tenor: Christ, on the point of leaving this world, gave us the memory or monument of himself, and nothing in the nature of that great monument obliged Christ to institute it after the event. The monument is such that he could erect it before the event, it being a sacrament. The institution of the Eucharistic sacrament of the Last Supper was not so much Christ's vow to die, as Christ's anticipated triumph in his death.

CHAPTER XV

S THOMAS AND THE COUNCIL OF TRENT ON THE ONENESS OF THE CHRISTIAN SACRIFICE

IF it is a maxim in the history of religious thought that no error ever achieves success except through the amount of truth on which it feeds, at no time was this more evident than when the reformers started preaching the uselessness of the Eucharistic sacrifice. Their success came from the most permanent of Christian truths, the all-sufficiency of the sacrifice of the cross. It became imperative, then, in the Catholic counter-reformation to investigate more deeply the relationship between the sacrifice of the cross and the Eucharistic sacrifice. The results of that great labour of investigation and restatement are embodied in the first and second chapters of the twenty-second Session of the Council of Trent. The remarkable feature, however, of that most scholarly and exact presentment of the Catholic doctrine of the Eucharistic sacrifice by the Fathers of Trent is this, that it gives an exact reproduction of the doctrine of S Thomas, whose line of thought and whose very expressions are easily recognised in the more classical treatment of the subject by the great Council.

One famous article of the *Summa* is obviously embodied in the above-mentioned conciliar pronouncement. It is the first Article of the eighty-third Question, " Whether Christ be immolated in this sacrament " (" Utrum in hoc sacramento Christus immolatur ").

I shall first give the text of S Thomas with the necessary comments, and then the words of the Council. Taken in conjunction, the two authorities, so distant in time, will make it clear for us how the Eucharist is a sacrifice, and is one and the same sacrifice with that of the cross.

" My answer is that the celebration of the sacrament is called an immolation of Christ for a twofold reason: firstly, indeed, because, according to Augustine in his letter to Simplicianus: ' The images of things bear the names of the things of which they are images; so that if we look at a picture or at a painted wall we say: " This one is Cicero, that one is Sallust." ' The celebration of the sacrament, then . . . is a certain image representative of the passion of Christ which is his true immolation; and therefore the celebration of the sacrament is called Christ's immolation. . . . In another way the celebration of the sacrament is called an immolation of Christ, on account of the effect of Christ's passion, because through this sacrament we become partakers of the fruits of Christ's passion. For this reason, in a certain *oratio secreta* of a Sunday, we say: ' As often as the commemoration of this victim is celebrated the work of our redemption is accomplished.' As far, then, as the first mode is concerned, it could be said that Christ was immolated also in the figures of the Old Testament; there are the words of Apocalypse xiii: ' Whose names are not written in the book of life of the Lamb which was slain from the beginning of the world.' But as far as the second mode is concerned, it belongs properly to this sacrament that in its celebration Christ be immolated ' (' Sed quantum ad secundum modum, proprium est huic sacramento, quod in ejus celebratione Christus immoletur ')."*

I quote the Latin of the last sentence because a certain amount of misunderstanding has surrounded this text. It is evident, after a careful perusal of the words of S Thomas, that he makes immolation in the Eucharist conterminous with representation and application. He makes a distinction, however, between representation

* III, Q. lxxxiii, Art. i.

and application, because application could only belong to the sacrament of the New Law, whilst representation may be predicated also òf the sacraments of the Old Law, though, of course, in a much more shadowy manner. The sacrament of the Old Law could never share in that thing which is called sacramental application; this is proper and exclusive to the sacrament of the New Law. S Thomas here repeats the doctrine enunciated in the former article*— namely, that the death of Christ being the efficient cause of salvation, it could not be applied to us except through the very fact of Christ having existed and having died in reality; a mere hope of a coming Christ could not be a *causa efficiens* applicable to the soul through real contact. S Thomas does not make a distinction between representation and application to the extent of causing a difference in the concept of Eucharistic immolation; all he means to say is this, that the kind of immolation which is conterminous with application could never be found outside the sacrament of the New Law, whilst the immolation, which is conterminous with representation, may be found, at least in a shadowy way, in the Jewish rites. In the sacrament of the Eucharist, then, representa-

* III, Q. lxii, Art. vi.

tion and application of the sacrifice of the cross
are the only kind of immolation to be admitted
in the sacrifice of the Christian altar. The
cross is Christ's true immolation. Mass is its
perfect image; therefore it is an immolation.
The Latin of S Thomas which expresses this
could not be more terse: " Celebratio autem
hujus sacramenti . . . imago quaedam est re-
praesentativa passionis Christi, quae est vera
ejus immolatio; et ideo celebratio hujus sacramenti dicitur Christi immolatio."*

S Thomas knew those very objections which
a few centuries later became such terrific issues.
Is it not strange how at one period men formulate
objections and their faith is not impaired, whilst
at another time the same difficulties, in no wise
more acute, become battle-cries of a spiritual
revolution ?

The first objection is as follows: " It would
seem that in the celebration of the sacrament
Christ is not immolated, for it is said in the
tenth chapter of the Hebrews that Christ ' by
one oblation has perfected for ever them that
are sanctified.' Now such an oblation was his
immolation. Christ, therefore, is not immolated in the celebration of the sacrament."
Protestantism has not formulated anything more

* III, Q. lxxxiii, Art. i.

definite against the Eucharistic sacrifice. Let us hear the answer. " S Ambrose . . . says: ' One is the victim ' which indeed Christ offered up and which we offer up, ' and the victims are not many, because Christ was offered up once.' Now this sacrifice is exemplary of that one. For as the thing which is offered up everywhere is one body and not many bodies, so there is also one sacrifice."

Here S Thomas gives the intrinsic and final reason to the oneness of the Christian sacrifice. The Body which is offered up is one and the same everywhere, be it on the cross, be it on the Christian altar. The sacrifice of Calvary and the sacrifice of the Eucharist are to each other in the relationship of the *exemplum;* one is the replica of the other. One contains what the other contains.

The second objector says: " The immolation of Christ was accomplished on the cross on which he delivered himself an oblation and a sacrifice to God for an odour of sweetness, as is said in the fifth chapter of the Ephesians; but in the celebration of this mystery Christ is not crucified, therefore he is not immolated." The answer of S Thomas shows how very little he was prepared to make any concessions to any kind of realistic crucifixion or the like in

Christ's own natural self in the Eucharistic sacrifice. " I say that as the celebration of the sacrament is the representative image of the passion of Christ, so is the altar representative of the cross itself on which Christ has been immolated in his own nature. . . ." Repre sentation here again makes the equation between cross and altar.

The third objection goes one step further. Quoting S Augustine, the objector says that in the immolation of Christ the priest and the victim are the same; now in the representation of the sacrament the priest and the victim are not the same; therefore the celebration of the sacrament could never be an immolation of Christ. Now for the answer. " In the same line of thought the priest also is the image of Christ, in whose person and by whose power he pronounces the words which make the con-secration . . . and so in a certain way the priest and the victim are the same." This answer carries the representative character of the Eucharistic immolation to the last degree of reality. In the Eucharist we have even that which made Christ's natural immolation so remarkable that the priest and the victim were the same. For in the Eucharist the priest and the victim are the same in sacramental sameness, as on Calvary they were the same in natural sameness. We see here how S Thomas differs in a way from more modern presentments of the same subject. For S Thomas there are two representative elements, the Christian priest and the sacramental Body and Blood. The priest represents Christ; the Eucharistic elements represent Christ's Body and Blood. The more modern way has been different; it says that Christ himself in his own Person is the priest who officiates at the altar as he officiated on Calvary. The way of S Thomas is, of course, more in keeping with the whole sacramental doctrine, as the Christian priesthood is as truly representative of Christ's priesthood as the Eucharistic Body is representative of Christ's natural Body.

The Christian priesthood is as truly a sacrament as the Christian sacrifice is a sacrament. The two sacraments stand to each other in the relation in which Christ stood to his immolation on the cross. Sacramentally the Catholic priesthood is one with the Eucharistic victim as, naturally, Christ was one with the thing he offered on the cross. But of this more will follow later on.

Let us now come to the text of the Council of Trent. We are dealing with a Latin style very different from the simple and direct phraseology of S Thomas; yet the ideas and many of the words of the angelic Doctor are to be found in the classical document without any disguise. We must, however, split up the phrase of the Renaissance Latin into its constituent parts with a certain amount of liberty, as it is intricate far beyond our modern directness of style. On the whole, in our talk we resemble more closely S Thomas than the Renaissance divines.

" Our God and Lord, who was on the point of offering himself on the Altar of the Cross to the Eternal Father through death, with a view of bringing about their eternal redemption, at the Last Supper on the night in which he was being betrayed, offered up to God the Father his Body and his Blood under the appearance of bread and wine. This he did in order not to let his priesthood come to an end through death, and thus he gave to his beloved Bride, the Church, a visible sacrifice in keeping with the exigencies of the nature of man. His object was this, that the bloody sacrifice which was on the point of being accomplished on the Cross should be represented; that its memory should remain to the end of the world, and that its saving power should be applied (to us) unto remission of those sins which are committed by us daily; and in acting thus he declared himself to be constituted a priest according to the order of Melchisedech for ever.

" Moreover, he gave his Body and Blood under the symbols of the same things to his Apostles for their food, making them then priests of the same New Testament. Furthermore, he gave them a precept to offer up in sacrifice his Body and Blood, and in their name to their successors in the priesthood. This precept was conveyed in the following words: ' Do this in memory of me.' Such has always been the understanding and the doctrine of the Catholic Church. After celebrating that old Pasch which the multitude of the Children of Israel were wont to immolate in memory of their flight from Egypt, Christ instituted the new Pasch, namely himself, to be immolated by the Church, through her priests under visible signs, in memory of his own passage from the world to the Father, that passage in which he redeemed us through the pouring out of his Blood and delivered us from the power of darkness and translated us into his kingdom. . . . And as in this divine sacrifice which is celebrated at Mass the very same Christ is contained and immolated in a bloodless fashion who had offered himself up once on the Altar of the

Cross in a bloody manner, it is the doctrine of this holy Synod that this sacrifice (of Mass) is truly the sacrifice of propitiation; for the Lord being appeased by the oblation of the sacrifice, giving grace and the gift of penance, remits the most heinous crimes and sins; for it is one and the same victim; the same is offering now through the ministry of the priests who then offered himself on the Cross, the difference being only in the way of offering. Of that offering, I mean the bloody offering, the fruits come to us most abundantly through the other offering (the unbloody one); so nothing is further away (from the mind of the Church) than that the one should be in the least way derogatory to the other.

"For this reason it is offered up, not only for the sins of the living faithful, their guilt, their satisfaction, and their other necessities, but it is also offered for those who died in Christ and who are not yet fully cleansed, and we do this legitimately, according to the tradition of the Apostles."

We have, then, in this passage of the Council, the words on which we have to ring the changes so often in this matter—representation, application, immolation, containing, and memory or even monument.

The Council accepts that duality which

S Thomas accepts. The sacrifice of the Cross is an absolutely complete act, and the sacrifice of Mass, again, is a complete act. The oneness of the Christian sacrifice is found in perfect representation, application, and containing. I do not insist on a further comparison between the conciliar passage and the article of S Thomas, on which we have already commented in this chapter; the resemblances are too obvious to need emphasising. Let me only remark that the Council makes it quite clear that the Last Supper was a complete act, representative by anticipation of that other complete act, the sacrifice of the first Good Friday. There is not a vestige in Tridentine mentality of those recent theories which make the Last Supper part of the whole sacrifice; in fact, one wonders how, in the face of such clear pronouncements, anyone could have the courage to disturb the traditional order of the redemptive dispensation—*i.e.*, first the institution of the commemorative sacrifice; second, the natural sacrifice; third, the celebration, no longer by Christ, but by the priest, of the commemorative sacrifice. The Council of Trent makes the Calvary sacrifice and the Eucharistic sacrifice to be one because it keeps them so well apart in their respective modes of being.

" The sacrifice which is offered daily in the Church is not something different from the sacrifice which Christ offered himself, but it is its memory."* Before the great Protestant controversies S Thomas, without peril of being misunderstood, could still make that extremely clear distinction between the sacrifice on the cross and its memory on the altars of the Church. Mass, for him, is a *commemoratio*. It is the radical distinction between the sacrifice of the cross and the sacrifice of the Eucharist, but we know what S Thomas meant by *commemoratio*. The question at issue is not whether it be a *commemoratio*, but what kind of *commemoratio* it be.

* III, Q. xxii, Art. iii ad 2m.

CHAPTER XVI

THE SACRIFICE OF THE CROSS

MY readers may be surprised to have been kept waiting until now for the one great thing round which all this matter of the Eucharist centres, the sacrifice of the cross—in other words, Christ's natural sacrifice. Would it not have been a more helpful method to make of this all-important point our very first chapter, since we have not been able so far to write a single page without referring to the sacrifice of the cross? This book, let me say it once more, is for the believer to whom the idea of the sacrifice of the cross is familiar; its object is to help us to visualise the Eucharist in its true setting; the cross is the centre more truly than the beginning of the sacramental system; there is, accordingly, no lack of good theological tactics if we pass through many a doctrinal rampart before we come to the great citadel which dominates everything, the mystery of Christ's sacrifice on Calvary. We have spoken of that mystery very often already, now we come to face it directly, and we gaze at it in its native beauty, after having loved its reflections all through the sacramental realm.

It is usual in modern theology to debate extensively on the nature of sacrifice in an abstract manner, and to apply those *a priori* conclusions on the essence of sacrifice to the Christian sacrifice, both natural and sacramental. It is remarkable, however, that amongst the many theological labours of S Thomas there is no such investigation into the nature of sacrifice. He does not seem to have felt the need of it. What he says of sacrifice in the earlier parts of the *Summa* is part of his theology on the virtue of religion, as religion, again, is part of the moral virtue of justice. He remains extremely sober in his zeal for investigating the nature of the sacrifice. I do not think I am alone in feeling that the theology of the Christian sacrifice has gained very little from the modern speculations on the nature of sacrifice in general.

The Christian sacrifice stands by itself with its own rites, and we know best what a sacrifice really is from the inspired literature of our Scriptures. It would certainly be a dangerous thing to formulate a theory of the sacrifice quite independent of that immense sacrificial life which has gone on for thousands of years under God's sanction and direction, and to apply such formulas to the divinely instituted sacrifices. It would be an attempt to explain the greater thing by the smaller, the divine thing by the human thing; certainly no theory of sacrifice could ever adequately meet the case of Christ's sacrifice on the cross. It is a sacrifice that has to be defined by itself and in itself.

We know from our Scriptures that the sacrifice is a mode of divine worship which is absolute, in the sense that God alone may be honoured in such a mode. We know, again from our Scriptures, that in many sacrifices there is destruction of the living organism, though there be sacrifices without such destruction. There is in a sacrifice this all-important element, which we overlook so often, the prearranged acceptance of God. God is willing to receive a definite homage; man will never be able to win God's favour through mere slaughterings of his precious herds; the sacrifice must be a covenanted thing between God and man. This most important factor ought to be enough to make us wary in laying down *a priori* maxims on the nature of sacrifice. There is, moreover, this complication, if I may use the word, that the whole ancient sacrificial rite was figurative of Christ's sacrifice on the cross. This means that we are to explain the ancient sacrifices through the sacrifice of the cross and not *vice versa*. We are dealing truly with the supernatural, the divinely established, the divinely revealed, in this whole matter of the sacrifice, and the speculations of natural theology ought to be subservient to the rite revealed by God himself.

There is in the sacrifices of the Levitic legislation a definiteness of procedure which has all the nature of a sacramental institution. We have heard S Thomas more than once speak of the ancient sacrifices as sacraments. They are extremely limited, both in ceremonial and in time; not any kind and every kind of man's generosity in God's service deserves the name of sacrifice. They are truly institutional religion, in the good sense of that much-abused word, because they are independent as forms of religion from subjective enthusiasm of religious feeling. They have a merit of their own, a power of pleasing God described in the oldest ritual phrases in the religious language of the world; they are essentially " a most sweet savour in the sight of the Lord, because it is his oblation."* This expression, " savour of sweetness," runs through the whole sacrificial

* Exod. xxix 25.

theology of the ancient law. It is a phrase of such fixity, recurring so often, that in it we evidently have the true meaning of sacrifice. The victim itself sends up to heaven a perfume of sweetness which is pleasing to the Lord God Almighty. " And Noe built an altar unto the Lord: and taking of all cattle and fowls that were clean, offered holocausts upon the altar. And the Lord smelled a sweet savour."*

Some people might be tempted to accuse the whole sacrificial theology of the Bible of materialism. There is certainly a definite material preciseness in the divinely instituted sacrifices of the past, and that very " odour of sweetness " which ascends to God from the burnt offering is a revelation to us of God's ways and preferences.

If I may philosophise in my turn, let me say that a sacrifice is an act of religion, and therefore an act of justice, rendering to God the thing due to God. It is not directly an act of fortitude or of temperance or of prudence; but it is a simple act of fair and just dealing with God, when man, or even the beast, is made to recognise God's sovereignty over all flesh. Even an heroic deed of fortitude in the service of God is not necessarily a sacrifice. A sacrifice need

* Gen. viii, 20, 21.

not be a difficult thing, or a painful thing, but it must be a just thing and a true thing, giving God the things that are God's, in the manner in which God wants to receive them back.

To spiritualise the sacrifice and to make of it exclusively an act of the created will or of the created mind would be the abolition of the sacrifice; all sacrifices are of the things that are bodily.

The great hieratic phrase " the odour of sweetness " is applied by S Paul to Christ on the cross: " Christ also hath loved us and hath delivered himself for us, an oblation and a sacrifice to God for an odour of sweetness."* We need hardly defend the old Christian tradition, as it has not really suffered any diminution in all the great religious upheavals that have rent Christianity, I mean the belief that Christ's death on the cross is a perfect and complete sacrifice, and that Christ is a High Priest through offering himself a victim to God on the cross. To give to Christ's crucifixion and death only moral worth, even if that worth be of an infinite degree, is not the whole of Christianity; there is something besides the moral worth of the suffering and dying Christ, there is the sacrifice.

* Eph. v 2.

Christ's death on the cross was truly a ritual act, as it was done at the time, in the manner, with the circumstances, ordained by the Father, and foreshadowed by all the ancient sacrifices. To make of the crucified Christ anything less than a victim, in the ceremonial sense of the word, is to bring down his death to the human plane.

My purpose in this chapter is not so much to establish the sacrificial nature of the crucifixion—how can any Catholic doubt it after a tradition of two thousand years?—as to show the definiteness and the bodily nature of that sacrifice. There is a clear danger besetting us in our own days, that of over-spiritualising the Incarnation and its circumstances, of attaching value only to such things in Christ as may be called his spiritual acts. The sacrifice of the cross is not primarily definable in terms of spirit, but in terms of the body; it is not the heroic fortitude of Christ on the cross which constitutes the sacrifice, but the material fact— we need not hesitate to use the word—of the pouring out of the Blood. There is in the sacrifice of the cross, as well as in the ancient sacrifices, an element of absolute stability, the Body of the victim; and from that there rises to heaven the odour of sweetness. The more perfect sacrifice is the one which is of the holier and cleaner body; and if we have a Body of infinite holiness, and of a cleanness absolutely divine, we have the sacrifice of infinite worth.

Let us hear S Thomas describing those qualities of Christ's flesh which make it a most perfect sacrifice. An objector says that Christ's passion on the cross ought not to be considered in the light of a sacrifice, because human flesh was never offered up in the ancient sacrifices, which were all of them the figure of Christ. As on the cross we have only Christ's flesh as a possible sacrifice, are we not compelled to drop entirely the idea of sacrifice out of the crucifixion? Such is the drift of the objector's argument, if not his very words. Now for the answer: " Although the reality ought to correspond with the prototype from a certain point of view, this need not be so from every point of view, because the reality ought to be greater than the type. It is, therefore, quite in order that the figure of the sacrifice (on the cross), through which the flesh of Christ is offered for us, was not the flesh of men, but of other animals by which was signified the flesh of Christ, which, indeed, is the most perfect sacrifice. Firstly, indeed, because being a flesh belonging to the human nature, it is offered up with great congruity for men, and is partaken of by them under the sacrament. Secondly, being a passible and a mortal flesh it was apt to be immolated. Thirdly, being a flesh without sin, it had efficacy for washing away sins. Fourthly, being the very flesh of the one who was offering it up, it was acceptable to God on account of the unspeakable charity of the one who thus offered his flesh. For this reason S Augustine says in the fourth Book of the Trinity: ' Is there anything more fitly taken by men and more fitly offered up for men, than human flesh ? Is there anything more apt for immolation than mortal flesh ? Is there anything so clean, with such power of cleansing away the sins of men as that flesh, born in a womb without the least stain of carnal lust, nay, born in the womb of a Virgin ? And can anything be offered up with such grace and be accepted with such grace as the flesh of our sacrifice, which has become the body of our priest ?' "*

S Augustine, the idealist, and S Thomas, the solid realist, are at one in their worship of Christ's flesh as being the most perfect sacrifice.

Are we, then, to separate, as it were, in that furnace of charity the passion and death of Christ, the physical element from the spiritual

* III, Q. xlviii, Art. iii ad 1m.

element, and are we to give the role of sacrifice
to the flesh by a real appropriation ? S Thomas
boldly makes this separation. The *Passio
Christi* works out our salvation, not in one way
only, but in five ways: by way of merit, by
way of satisfaction, by way of sacrifice, by way
of redemption, and by way of efficiency. The
whole Quaestio xlviii of the Third Part of the
Summa is a study of wonderful acumen of
those five ways by which we are saved. The
question arises, are they only five different
aspects of one and the same thing—in other
words, is sacrifice the same thing as merit, as
satisfaction, as redemption ? S Thomas seems
to keep them well apart. " The passion of
Christ, from the point of view of Christ's
divinity, acts by way of efficiency; from the
point of view of the will and Christ's soul, it
acts by way of merit; but from the point of view
of that thing, Christ's flesh, it acts by way of
satisfaction, as far as through the passion we
are liberated from the burden of punishment;
it acts by way of redemption as far as through
the passion we are set free from the slavedom
of guilt; but it acts by way of sacrifice inasmuch
as through the passion we are reconciled unto
God " (" Passio Christi, secundum quod comparatur ad divinitatem ejus, agit per modum

efficientiae: inquantum vero comparatur ad voluntatem animae Christi, agit per modum meriti: secundum vero quod consideratur in ipsa carne Christi, agit per modum satisfactionis, inquantum per eam liberamur a reatu poenae; per modum vero redemptionis, inquantum per eam liberamur a servitute culpae; per modum autem sacrificii, inquantum per eam reconciliamur Deo ").*

S Thomas evidently makes Christ's flesh the bearer of that wonderful mission, the sacrificial mission. All things in Christ's passion were not directly sacrifice, because there were mighty things of the spirit, which, being of the spirit, could not be properly called sacrifice; not in his Spirit, but in his flesh did Christ feel the burden that was put on him by the Father. "The spirit indeed is willing, but the flesh is weak."†

Though we may separate the elements of sacrifice in Christ's passion from the other elements, we do not, of course, isolate it. Everything that constitutes the sanctity and the holiness of the victim is a direct addition to the value of the sacrifice. But it is certain, from all theological principles, that not all of Christ's activity here on earth has in any way the property of sacrifice. His long life in poverty at Nazareth is decidedly not the sacrifice of the New Law

* III, Q. xlviii, Art. vi ad 3m.   † Matt. xxvi 41.

THE SACRIFICE OF THE CROSS

His Baptism and his fast, his patient endurance
of persecution during his three years of public
life, are not the sacrifice of the New Law. So
much is admitted by the consensus of Catholic thought. The further distinction which
S Thomas seems to make and which I have
quoted, analyses, so to speak, Christ's passion
itself, and separates the sacrificial elements from
the non-sacrificial elements even in that supreme
moment of Christ's career. But all that previous
sanctity, all the charity of the cross, were
focussed on that one element, sacrifice, because
they made the victim holy beyond words. If
they were not the sacrifice they were the sanctity
of the victim, they were the glory of that life
which was to be laid down in the sacrifice, and
the higher the life, the more precious the laying
down of it and the greater the sacrifice.

Another passage of S Thomas which clearly
distinguishes even in the passion, of Christ
between sacrifice and other cleansing powers
of that great fight of the Son of God against
evil, is found in the fourth Article of the forty-
ninth Question, " Whether through the passion
of Christ we have been reconciled to God ?"

" My answer is that the passion of Christ is
the cause of our reconciliation with God in a
twofold manner: in one way because it takes

away sin through which men are made enemies of God. . . . In another way through its being a sacrifice most acceptable unto God, for this is properly the effect of a sacrifice that through it God be appeased."

A simple consideration will make it clear to the least initiated how in that infinitely great thing, the passion of Christ, sacrifice must be distinguished from other things. Mankind as a race has been redeemed once for all by Christ's death on the cross; the power of Satan has been broken as a monarchy of evil. Now this redemption cannot be repeated, even sacramentally, because it is not applicable to individual souls, but it is concerned with the whole of mankind. It lies, so to speak, at the basis of all other dealings of God with men. Very often the terms " redemption," " satisfaction," and " sacrifice " are interchanged, as, indeed, they are so closely united in that one central thing, the passion of Christ; and it is said commonly that we are redeemed through Christ's sacrifice on the cross. But precision becomes necessary when we are anxious to see everything in its proper setting, and sacrifice, even of the cross, is not quite the same thing as redemption of the cross. " To be saved " may be considered as the most universal result of the cross. Salvation, in the doctrine of S Thomas, is through five different ways.

Christ merited for himself that supreme exaltation of which S Paul speaks in the Epistle to the Philippians: " He humbled himself, becoming obedient unto death, even to the death of the cross. For which cause, God also hath exalted him, and hath given him a name which is above all names."* Here, again, we have an element in Christ's passion which cannot be strictly described under the heading " sacrifice," as S Thomas points out so clearly in the twenty-second Question of Part Three, in Article four. An objector says that Christ's death on the cross was beneficial to himself, because through the cross Christ merited exaltation for himself. This S Thomas clearly denies, quoting the Council of Ephesus, which excommunicates anyone who says that Christ offered up sacrifices for himself. Christ's priesthood and Christ's sacrifice are all for the benefit of man. This gives S Thomas another occasion for making a distinction in the glories of the cross, discriminating glory from glory: " In the offering of the sacrifice by every priest we may consider two things—namely, the sacrifice itself, which is offered, and the zeal of the one

* Phil. ii 8, 9.

171

who offers. Now the real effect of a priesthood
is the one that comes from the sacrifice itself.
But Christ merited through his passion the
glory of the Resurrection, not in virtue of the
sacrifice which is offered up by way of atonement, but through that zeal of his through
which he bore his passion with such humility,
according to charity " (" Christus autem con-
secutus est per suam passionem gloriam resur-
rectionis, non quasi ex vi sacrificii, quod offertur
per modum satisfactionis, sed ex ipsa devotione,
qua secundum charitatem humiliter passionem
sustinuit ").*

We may, then, without further entering into
that matter, take it for granted that even in the
passion there were definite things that constituted the sacrifice, and these definite things
are represented directly in the Eucharistic
sacrifice.

The very nature of sacrifice implies a gift to
God, and this aspect of gift is the one constantly
mentioned by S Thomas when he distinguishes
sacrifice from the other splendours of Christ's
passion. " This is properly the effect of a
sacrifice that through it God be appeased, as
even man is ready to forgive an injury done
unto him by accepting a gift which is offered to

* III, Q. xxii, Art. iv ad 2m.

him. Thus it is said in the First Book of Kings in the twenty-sixth chapter: 'If the Lord stir thee up against me, let him accept of sacrifice.' And so in the same way what Christ suffered was so great a good that, on account of that good found in human nature, God has been appeased over all the offences of mankind, anyhow with regard to those who are linked up with the Christ who suffered, in the way mentioned before."*

The feature in the passion which seems especially the gift of Christ to his Father, and which therefore is more particularly the element of sacrifice, is the laying down of his life: "Therefore doth the Father love me: because I lay down my life that I may take it again. No man taketh it away from me: but I lay it down of myself. And I have power to lay it down: and I have power to take it up again. This commandment have I received of my Father."† And this laying down of the life is the same as the pouring out of his life-blood. So we see S Paul, in the Epistle to the Hebrews, making the sacrifice of the cross consist in the Blood. The texts are well known; they are truly a hymn of Christ's great sacrifice on the

* III, Q. xlix, Art. iv.
† John x 17. 18.

173

cross. " But Christ, being come an high priest of the good things to come, by a greater and more perfect tabernacle, not made with hand, that is, not of this creation: neither by the blood of goats or of calves, but by his own blood, entered once into the Holies, having obtained eternal redemption. For if the blood of goats and of oxen and the ashes of an heifer, being sprinkled, sanctify such as are defiled, to the cleansing of the flesh: how much more shall the blood of Christ, who by the Holy Ghost offered himself unspotted to God, cleanse our conscience from dead works, to serve the living God ? And therefore is he the mediator of the new testament: that by means of his death for the redemption of those transgressions which were under the former testament, they that are called may receive the promise of eternal inheritance. . . . Nor yet that he should offer himself often, as the high priest entereth into the Holies every year with the blood of others. For then he ought to have suffered often from the beginning of the world. But now once, at the end of ages, he hath appeared for the destruction of sin by the sacrifice of himself. And, as it is appointed unto men once to die, and after this the judgement; so also Christ was offered once to exhaust the sins of many. The second time he shall appear without sin to them that expect him unto salvation."*

Much could be said on these inspired words; but if they make clear one thing it is this, the sacrificial nature of the passion of Christ, and, above all, the sacrificial nature of the pouring out of the Blood. This latter feature in Christ's passion seems to be the supreme sacerdotal act, and no doubt it is there we must find the essence of the great Christian sacrifice.

This is the thing represented in the Eucharist; this was the thing foreshadowed in all the sacrifices of the Old Law.

We have come to elements which are clearly traceable, as you may trace the course of a river which springs from the mountains, then passes through a lake, and comes out of the lake on its long course towards the ocean, through the cities of men. The first portion of the stream we may identify with the figurative sacrifice of the Old Law; the lake, with the stream clearly moving through it, even with a diversity in the colour of the water, is the sacrificial element in Christ's glorious passion; the third, and the longest stretch of the river, is the Eucharistic sacrifice.

* Heb. ix 11-15 and 25-28.

CHAPTER XVII

TRANSUBSTANTIATION

NOTHING could give us a clearer insight into the Eucharistic doctrine than the position which Transubstantiation holds in the Eucharist. We have already quoted S Thomas (P. III, Q. lxxviii, Art. iv) telling us that the power which changes comes after the power of signification; in other words, the whole external sacramental action in words and deeds signifies one thing, and one thing only, the Body of Christ and the Blood of Christ. This is the oldest form under which we meet the Eucharist in Christian tradition. The Church has simply given a literal interpretation to the words of the Eucharistic rite. It was not said first that bread was being changed into Christ's Body and that wine was being changed into Christ's Blood; what was said first and is said at all times, is: " This is my Body, this is my Blood "; the additional concept of change may be truly called an after-thought.

The Church could not give the reason of her great sacramental utterances without giving for her explanation this mysterious change which is so near to the heart of the main mystery itself that it may truly be called a part of it. The substance of bread is changed into Christ's Body and the substance of wine is changed into Christ's Blood. Transubstantiation, then, is not so much the sacrament, as the divinely revealed explanation of the truth of the sacrament; Transubstantiation is not the Eucharistic sacrifice, but it is the hidden power that makes the sacrifice a reality, not a mere symbol.

An instance from another portion of Catholic theology makes this relative position of Transubstantiation in the Eucharistic mystery quite comprehensible.

Catholic theology holds that God creates directly every human soul, and unites it with the human embryo. Now this doctrine of God's direct creative act in producing the soul is not a doctrine that stands in the first rank of truths; but it is a doctrine which has to be brought in as the only satisfactory hypothesis in the explanation of man's nature. A doctrine that stands in the first rank of evidence is this, that man, as we know him, is endowed with an intellectual soul; this is the thing that matters to us, and which is evident to us in its own directness of proof. Yet when we come to ask the question, How is this intellectual principle found in man? the only answer is this: God creates it in every instance. So it is with Transubstantiation. The doctrine that stands in the first rank of evidence is the Body and Blood of Christ given to us in the form of sacri-fice. This is the mystery we approach at once; we enter into it directly; nothing prepares us for it except the authority of Christ and his Church. In matters of the Eucharist we truly enter at once *in medias res;* so to speak, we stumble without any preparation on the sacra-ment of Christ's Body and Christ's Blood. The holiest thing is the first thing we meet. We do not bring Christ down from heaven; we do not raise him up from the depths through the sacra-mental signification; he is in our hands and in our mouths before we know where we are. The sacrifice is consummated through the lightning power of the sacramental words that announce it. Overawed, as it were, by the might of the thing that has happened, we ask: How did it happen? The answer is, Tran-substantiation. As in the case of the human personality shining in power of intellect, and showing forth a splendid soul, the unseen fiat of God in a mother's womb is the only satis-factory hypothesis at the root of that splendour of personality which meets me in the human being, perfect in mind and body, so is Transubstantiation at the root of the Eucharistic blessings.

Transubstantiation, then, is not, and could not be, the same thing as the Eucharist, both in its aspect of sacrifice and food; but it is at the root of the sacrament, deep down in the abyss of being, where God's omnipotence is supreme.

Theologians sometimes, more devout than learned, have given this visualising of the Eucharistic sacrifice. In every sacrifice, they said, the first thing is the bringing in of the victim; then there is the consecration of the victim; and thirdly there is its immolation. They thought that Transubstantiation could be made to answer exactly for the first stage of a sacrifice, the bringing in of a victim, as, through it, Christ's Body and Christ's Blood were brought to our altars. But who does not see how infelicitous a role Transubstantiation is thus given? It places it in the first rank of sacramental truth, instead of making it the explanation of sacramental truth. In such a theory Transubstantiation would be the sacrament itself, and we should have for sacrament, not a divine thing, but the act of God in itself, because Transubstantiation is the act of God. It is as if we made that act by which he creates every individual soul part and parcel of the individual nature of the men whom we meet. This, of course, would be an unpardonable confusion of thought. Let us say it once more, Transubstantiation is not the same thing as the sacrament of Christ's Body and Christ's Blood; those things we hold in virtue of sacramental formulas of consecration; but it is the hidden act of God, which is absolutely indispensable if the sacramental consecration be true.

There is a beautiful phrase of S Thomas in the seventy-fifth Question, Article two, *ad primum*. The article sets out to prove that the substance of bread and wine does not remain after the consecration: " God has yoked his divinity, that is to say, his divine power, to bread and wine, not so that they should remain in the sacrament, but so as to make from bread and wine his body and his blood " ("Deus conjugavit divinitatem suam, idest divinam virtutem, pani et vino, non ut remaneant in hoc sacramento, sed ut faciat inde corpus et sanguinem suum ").

The power we call Transubstantiation is a transient act, whilst the sacrament abides for a time, more or less prolonged. This power does not remain in the sacrament, but the Body and Blood of Christ remain. This consideration should be enough to make it clear to us what a difference there is between Transubstantiation and the sacrament properly so called; and to show what confusion would arise in our theological thinking if we made Transubstantiation at any time to stand for an element in the essence of the Eucharistic sacrifice.

After these considerations on the comparatively relative position of Transubstantiation in the Eucharistic doctrine, let us come now to a few aspects which will endear to us this divine thing, Transubstantiation, as being the most simple—nay, even the most beautiful explanation of all we know of the Eucharistic mystery. If it is not the sacrament itself, it is certainly the sweet and gracious mother of the sacrament. In its simplicity it has all the grace and charm of eternal wisdom.

The best way I know in order to make clear to the reader the glory of Transubstantiation is this assertion, that after Christ, the Son of God, had done the great deed of the first consecration at the Last Supper, the miracle was complete, and nothing new has happened since. The circumstance that thousands of priests consecrate to-day in all parts of the world is no new marvel.

Transubstantiation contained it all from the beginning. Transubstantiation is the power of Christ to change bread into his Body and wine into his Blood. Now this is an absolute power, not limited in any way. If the thing can be done once, it can be done always, in every place, wherever bread and wine are found. There are no fresh, no new difficulties, because the power of Transubstantiation is concerned directly with the whole species of bread and wine. If you admit once that Christ has power to raise up the dead, or if he has raised up a dead man once, you are not surprised if he raises up a hundred or a thousand or a million dead men; it is all the same to him, if he has power over death. It would, indeed, be a childish attitude of mind to think that it is more difficult for God to heal ten lepers than to heal one leper, to raise up ten dead men than to raise up one dead man. So with this power of Transubstantiation: if one piece of bread, if one cup of wine may be changed by Christ into his Body and his Blood, why not a hundred breads or a hundred cups ? The mystery is identical.

There is truly no more reason to be astonished at the number of Eucharistic sacrifices offered up than at the number of Baptisms administered in the world. If there is the power in the

Church to regenerate into spiritual life one soul
—and this power is a tremendous power, much
greater than we think—every soul may be
brought under the influence of Baptismal regeneration. If Christ, holding bread and the
cup of wine, could declare them to be the same
thing as the Body and the Blood that then were
constituent elements of his living Personality,
the same declaration may be repeated with the
same truthfulness, because the underlying power
remains unaltered, undiminished: this is Transubstantiation. Its wisdom, or, if you prefer,
the wisdom of the Church, in declaring Transubstantiation to be the only explanation she
has of her mystery of faith, may be seen more
clearly if we compare Transubstantiation with
another mode, a hypothetical one, of course,
which has been excogitated by thinkers, more
ardent, perhaps, than illumined, in order to
have a satisfactory answer to the question how
Christ is present on so many altars. They have
recourse to metaphysical theories on the nature
of space and place; they have said, in so many
words, that the Body of Christ could come into
every corner of the world simultaneously, as
possessing a kind of multiplicity of presence.
Such a theory, if it mean anything at all, would
certainly imply this one element, that Christ,

in his bodily nature, would be moving backward and forward in space with incredible rapidity so as to be present on every altar at the moment of consecration. This is a bewildering way of explaining the Real Presence, and the fact of its having been patronised by pious men does not make it less confusing. It would make of the Eucharist a thing of material mobility and velocity. Not so Transubstantiation. Where-ever a priest, in the virtue of Christ, pronounces the sacramental consecration, the substance of the bread and the substance of the wine are changed into that one thing, the substance of Christ's Body and the substance of Christ's Blood. There is no bringing down from heaven of the Body and Blood of Christ; this is not the Eucharist; but Christ's Body and Christ's Blood are truly produced in an act of divine power, as grace is produced in the human soul at Baptism. The thing produced in the Eucharist is, of course, wonderfully greater than that produced in Baptism; but in both cases it is a production—nay, in both cases it is a change. In Baptism the soul is changed from sin unto grace; in the Eucharist the substance of bread and the substance of wine are changed into the substance of Christ's Body, into the substance of Christ's Blood.

It is not only a change into a greater thing than Baptism, but it is also a greater change, because the whole reality is changed, down to the very roots of being; yet, let us repeat it, in both cases, in Baptism and in the Eucharist, the sacrament is a changing.

Multiplicity of the sacramental act, both in time and space, adds nothing to the sacrament. In the words of S Thomas, we do not say, or ought not to say, that Christ is on many altars, as in so many places, but as in the sacrament: " The body of Christ is not in this sacrament in the manner in which a body is in a place, having its dimensions rounded off by the place; but he is present in a certain special manner, which belongs exclusively to this sacrament; so we say that the body of Christ is on many altars, not as in so many places, but as in the sacrament; by which we do not mean that Christ is there only in a sign, although the sacrament be of the genus sign; but we understand that the body is there . . . according to the manner proper to the sacrament " (" Corpus Christi non est eo modo in hoc sacramento, sicut corpus in loco, quod suis dimensionibus loco commensuratur, sed quodam speciali modo, qui est proprius huic sacramento: unde dicimus, quod corpus Christi est in diversis altaribus, non sicut in diversis locis, sed sicut in sacramento: per quod non intelligimus, quod Christus sit ibi solum sicut in signo, licet sacramentum sit in genere signi; sed intelligimus corpus Christi hic esse, sicut dictum est . . . secundum modum proprium huic sacramento ").*

The uninitiated may be startled when he hears S Thomas declare that the Body of Christ in the sacrament is not in a place, as he is in heaven in a place; yet such is the emphatic and unswerving teaching of S Thomas. For the great Doctor it is simply unthinkable—nay, it implies a metaphysical contradiction—that the Body of Christ should ever be considered as moving simultaneously from place to place, or as overcoming, in some miraculous manner, all spatial hindrances. Transubstantiation is infinitely simpler. Wherever bread is found, wherever wine is found, their hidden substance is transubstantiated into the hidden substance of Christ's Body and Blood, in the same way in which it was done at the Last Supper. This is what S Thomas means when he says that the Body of Christ is not in a place but in a sacrament. The thing, the Body of Christ, is not taken hold of, hurried through space and put

* III, Q. lxxv, Art. i ad 3m.

into a definite place on a definite altar; this is not Eucharist at all; but the divine invocation, as the words of consecration are so often called by the Fathers, makes the substance of a definite bread and the substance of a definite cup of wine into a new thing, and what is that new thing? It is simply that thing which is in heaven, the Body and Blood of Christ, but which, not for one instant, has left heaven.

The usual term which makes the difference between the Catholic and the Protestant view of the Eucharist is " Real Presence." Christ's Body and Christ's Blood are really present—nay, the whole Christ is really present, as will be seen in a later chapter. But, confining ourselves to Body and Blood, they are present; yet we say with great attention to accuracy of thought that Christ is not on the altar as in a place. No doubt for most men to be present somewhere is the same thing as being placed there; there is, however, a vast difference. The bread and wine before the consecration are truly on the altar as in a place, they are put on the altar by the minister. What are called the accidents of bread and wine, the external appearances, remain on the altar during the sacrifice, even after the consecration. But there is a thing, an inward element of reality in that bread and wine which the sacramental consecration changes into a much greater reality, Christ's Body and Christ's Blood; and that change is the only reason why Christ is there.

Christ is on the altar as in a sacrament, according to the fine expression of S Thomas, in virtue of a hidden change within the nature of the bread and wine. Here we have the application in its sublimest form, that the sacrament produces the thing which it signifies; it signifies the Body and Blood of Christ, and it produces It.

As already insinuated, the difference between the Eucharist and the other sacraments is not one of kind, but one of degree. They are all of them powers of changing. In the other sacraments the change is in the soul of men, in this sacrament the change is in the very elements, bread and wine. Perhaps we think it a less difficult marvel, a lighter tax on our faith, that the soul of the infant, through Baptismal regeneration, should receive the life of God, the imprint of Christ, the likeness of the angels, than that bread and wine should be made into the holy thing that was on the cross, that was poured out on Calvary. But is it really a more incredible thing?

TRANSUBSTANTIATION

S Thomas speaks of the two marvels in the same breath, as if they were not essentially different, as if the one ought to prepare us for the other: " What the power of the Holy Ghost is with regard to the water of Baptism, this the true body of Christ is with regard to the appearances of bread and wine " (" Sicut autem se habet virtus Spiritus Sancti ad aquam baptismi, ita se habet corpus Christi verum ad speciem panis et vini ").* Once we admit that God dwells in material things as a source of eternal life—and this is the very concept of the Christian sacrament—have we not admitted the Eucharistic mystery, the Real Presence ? The thing which is Christ's Body and Christ's Blood is under the material appearances of bread and wine.

The Christian sacraments are infinitely fertile things. The material, the external sign in the word and element becomes fruitful beyond calculation in the realm of grace. Is it not an ancient metaphor with the Fathers to call the baptismal waters a mother's womb ? The Eucharistic sacrament is the most fertile of them, yet its fertility belongs to the same secret source of life.

The older mode of conceiving the Eucharist

* III, Q. lxxiii, Art. i ad 2m.

places itself exclusively at this angle of vision, the wonderful productiveness of power. Christ's Eucharistic Body is produced in the manner in which his divine hands produced bread when he multiplied the loaves. The older thinkers are not hampered by what might be called the spatial difficulty in the Eucharist; they saw no spatial difficulty, because there is none. The power of Christ to change bread and wine is the only thing they knew of, and their Eucharistic theology is, indeed, simple in the extreme, because they believed in the power of the sacrament to produce what it signifies.

Two simple metaphysical concepts of S Thomas may fitly conclude this chapter. There is in the metaphysical presentment of the Eucharist by S Thomas a wonderful calmness of outlook, and a complete avoidance of the worry of thought from which even good theologians have not always been able to escape. "Through the power of a finite agent no one form can be changed into another form, no one matter can be changed into another matter; but such a change can be effected through the power of an infinite agent, whose action extends over the whole realm of being. . . . What is being in one, the author of being may change into that which is being in another, by removing that which made the difference."* When S Thomas says that God has power over the whole realm of being he has truly given us the last word in this matter; and yet how simple this last word is: " Habet actionem in totum ens."

Another such serene utterance is concerned with the cessation of the sacramental presence. When the appearances of bread and wine lose their identity, as they do very rapidly—for the Eucharist, being a sacrament, is essentially of a transient nature—the Body and Blood also cease to be present. How do Body and Blood cease to be there? How does It depart? " The body of Christ remains in the sacrament, not only for the day after the consecration, but even for a future time, as long as the sacramental appearances remain. If they cease to be what they are, then the body of Christ ceases to be under them, not because the body of Christ depends on them (for its existence), but simply because the relationship of Christ's body to those appearances is taken away. In this manner God ceases to be the Lord of a creature whose existence ceases " (" Corpus Christi remanet in hoc sacramento, non solum in crastino, sed etiam in futuro, quousque species sacramentales manent, quibus cessanti-

* III, Q. lxxv, Art. iv ad 3m.

bus, desinit esse corpus Christi sub eis, non quia ab eis dependeat, sed quia tollitur habitudo corporis Christi ad illas species: per quem modum Deus desinit esse dominus creaturae desinentis ").*

May it not be said that the Eucharistic mystery is really no exception to those laws of being, both finite and infinite, created and increate, which Catholic theology has studied and enunciated with such success? But if, instead of metaphysics of being, we were to use sentiment and imagination in giving the account of our faith, should we not very soon find ourselves hopelessly entangled?

* III, Q. lxxvi, Art. vi ad 3m.

CHAPTER XVIII

EUCHARISTIC " DIFFICULTIES "

IT almost raises a smile when one sees the apparently casual way in which S Thomas treats the most burning of all spiritual questions: " Whether in the sacrament the body of Christ be according to truth."* It is by no means the first thing he asks; this great query comes almost in the middle of his treatment of the Eucharist. Till then he has been busy showing that the Eucharist is truly a sacrament; and it looks as if this question of questions were merely part of a chain of reasonings through which the true sacramental character of the Eucharist is established. For that purpose he has to prove the all-important circumstance that Christ's Body and Blood are in the sacrament, literally so, according to truth. There is, indeed, profound wisdom in such an arrangement, and no one who has given much time to that part of the *Summa* will ever say that the theology of S Thomas on the Eucharist is not complete. It is a monument of spiritual

* III, Q. lxxv, Art. i.

and mystical insight. But let us be quite frank on the subject, the monument is not a pyramid, standing in isolated greatness in the midst of the desert; the monument is the citadel which crowns the city, I mean the sacramental theology, which leads up to it and leads away from it.

After giving the reasons why the Body of Christ is in truth in the sacrament, he concludes: " Some men, not bearing in mind these reasons, say that the body and blood of Christ were in the sacrament only as in a sign; but this is to be rejected as heretical, it being contrary to .the words of Christ. And therefore Berengarius, who was the first author of such an error, has been obliged to recant his error and to make a profession of the truth of the faith."* When we remember what has happened since in the world round this very sacrament, the serenity of S Thomas produces a mild hilarity in the severest mind.

Human imagination rose one day like a giant who had been slumbering after excess of wine. It broke all it could, and filled the world with the ruins of the Catholic altars. Yet it is clear that not one of those difficulties which, a few centuries after S Thomas, sent a portion of the

* III, Q. lxxv, Art. i.

Western mind into a frenzy of denials and even blasphemies, was unknown in the days of the great thinker, or was undiscussed in all the schools of theology. In fact, the medieval way of stating such difficulties is astonishingly frank and complete. But at no time did the philosophers of the ages of faith come across one single thing that could be truly called an impossibility, or, as they would have named it, a *contradictio in terminis*, a contradiction, an incompatibility of concepts. There is great wisdom in their selection of the arena for the battle. For them the puzzles, if puzzles there were, had reference essentially—nay, exclusively —to the constitution of the material body.

Admitting the power of creation, it was no true difficulty to them that God should change any one thing into another thing; that he should change water into wine, or even bread and wine into any other substance: all this is implied in the concept of creative power. The departure from their normal thinking was in this one point that in this very change there is a selection of extraordinary penetration; in the same bodily thing one thing is changed and the other thing remains unchanged; again, the change results into a new thing, not in its complete material circumstances, but with a wonderful detachment from any material circumstances. Not the whole bread and the whole wine are changed, but the substance only of the bread and the substance only of the wine; what they call the accidents, the external appearances, remain and become solid realities in their own right.

Again, the Body of Christ and the Blood of Christ, which are the new thing after the Transubstantiation, are not there in the natural mode in which bodily things occupy room in spatial surroundings. This division of reality from reality is the only difficulty for the thinker; the change itself is admitted by implication the moment creation is admitted. All the thinking of the schoolmen in Eucharistic matters is concerned with change, not with space, as is too often the case in more recent treatment of the Eucharist. Now S Thomas frankly admits that in this change there are certain issues not contained in the ordinary principles of the doctrine of creation: " In this change there are several things which are more difficult than the things in creation, for in creation this alone is the difficulty, that something is made of nothing; but, after all, this is the proper manner of production belonging to the First Cause, which presupposes nothing else (on which to act). But in this change the difficulty lies not only in the circumstance that one being in its totality be changed into another being in its totality, so that nothing of the former being remains (which mode of production, indeed, is not usual with any cause), but there is the additional difficulty, that, namely, the accidents remain when the substance has been changed; and there are many other difficult matters of which we shall have to treat later on. We use, however, with regard to the sacrament, the word ' change,' not the word ' creation.' "* We know, of course, what S Thomas means when he uses the term *difficile*, ' difficult.' The difficulty is not on the part of God, but on the part of the human intellect. Besides that, nothing prepares bodily matter like bread and wine for a change at the same time so absolute and so discerning. For the power of the Creator, no doubt, this is a plaything, as everything else in the material world is a plaything: " This change takes place, not through any passive potentiality of the creature, but through the sole active power of the Creator " (" Non enim haec conversio fit per potentiam passivam creaturae, sed per solam potentiam activam creatoris ").†

If the Eucharistic doctrine of S Thomas takes anything for granted it is the wealth of

* III, Q. lxxv, Art. viii ad 3m.   † *Ibid.*, ad 4m.

reality contained under the least particle of a material thing. Modern science cannot, of course, prove that accidents and substances are separable things; but modern science has proved the inexhaustible wealth that is in every particle of matter.

The Catholic theologian, then, has to admit the difficulty; but let him put it in its proper place. No doubt his troubles are at bottom not greater than the troubles of anyone who tries to give a satisfactory reason to the power of the atom. Once more, I want to remind the reader that everything in the Eucharist, as in other sacraments, centres round the idea of change, either spiritual or material. Can our souls be changed through the baptismal waters and the Holy Ghost ? Can our wills be changed through the absolving power of penance ? Can the innermost portion of our spirit be changed ? Can it be sealed by the Holy Ghost in the sacrament of Confirmation ? These are mighty questions indeed. The Catholic Church answers them all in the affirmative. The Eucharistic change is concerned directly with the elements themselves. Can bread and wine be changed into a divine Thing ? Again the Church says: Yes. This is the difference between the Eucharist and the other sacraments, not a radical difference, but only an accidental difference. " This sacrament differs from the other sacraments in two ways: firstly, because this sacrament is completed in the consecration of the matter, whilst the other sacraments are completed in the use of the matter; secondly, because in the other sacraments the consecration of the matter is merely a certain blessing (bestowed upon them), . . . but in this sacrament the consecration of the matter consists in a certain miraculous change of the substance which can be accomplished by God alone."*

The receiving of the Eucharist by the faithful is, of course, an additional sacramental aspect. Protestantism has located the Eucharistic change in the soul only, when Christ is received by faith; Catholicism, with a deeper insight into spiritual realities, places the Eucharistic change, before all things and above all things, in the Eucharistic elements. After all, are the changes of the individual soul such an easy matter? Why do we believe more readily in the conversion of a sinner than in the Eucharistic change, which is constantly called by S Thomas a *conversio*? Did we know the real workings of things, perhaps we might find it just as difficult to believe in conversion as in Tran-

* III, Q. lxxviii, Art i.

substantiation, unless we had God's authority. Is there not a famous passage in the Gospels where our Lord himself appeals to God's omnipotence in order to explain moral conversion? "And Jesus seeing him (the young man) become sorrowful, said: How hardly shall they that have riches enter into the kingdom of God! For it is easier for a camel to pass through the eye of a needle than for a rich man to enter into the kingdom of God. And they that heard him said: Who, then, can be saved? He said to them: The things that are impossible with men are possible with God."*

In this matter of the Eucharist, as in all matters of theology, we should be satisfied with such aspects of the doctrine as the most exact mind accepts in all dutifulness of faith. This is particularly the case with the all-important question of the identity between Christ's natural Body and Christ's Eucharistic Body. This identity is no longer a difficulty of the material order, but it is really a point belonging directly to the metaphysics of being. In which sense must we say that the Eucharistic Body is identical with the natural Body of Christ? That they are identical is the very point of this sacrament; yet even in this identity there is

* Luke xviii 24-27.

a possibility of difference. Let us bear in mind that the Eucharistic Body of Christ is truly the result of a production, of a change. It is made; *conficitur* is the word used both in theology and the Liturgy. S Thomas is quite express in giving to the Eucharistic Body one *esse* and to Christ's natural Body another *esse*. " Christ has not the same *esse* in himself and the same *esse* under this sacrament, because when we say that he has an *esse* under the sacrament there is signified a relationship of himself to the sacrament " (" Christo autem non est idem esse secundum se, et esse sub hoc sacramento; quia per hoc quod dicimus ipsum sub hoc sacramento, significatur quaedam habitudo ejus ad hoc sacramentum ").*

It is difficult to render into English the full meaning of *esse*. " Mode of being " is perhaps the nearest approach to a complete rendering. With perfect identity in everything, there is still this possible difference, there is another mode of being. In the Eucharist we have the Body of Christ and the Blood of Christ, but with a mode of being entirely different from that mode of being in which Christ was at the Last Supper, in which he is now in heaven.

I may quote in conclusion from the theo-

* III, Q. lxxvi, Art. vi.

logians of Salamanca, who indisputably form one of the most orthodox schools of Catholic thought. In their great work on the Eucharist they say, with charming liberality of theological manners: " The opinion which one ought to prefer quite simply in this matter is the one which makes the thing more clear to the intellect, answering the difficulties which are brought forward. This is really the task assigned more particularly to a theologian in matters of such difficulty. This result we shall obtain, then, if we say that the term towards which the act of Transubstantiation tends is the Body and Blood of Christ, with a new substantial mode of being, a mode of being different from the one Christ has in heaven, a mode of being acquired (in the sacrament) through the change and in virtue of the change. . . . It is clear, then, that Christ, as he is in himself and as he is in heaven in his natural mode of being, is really distinct from himself in as far as he claims for himself and owns that substantial mode of being which he has in the sacrament."*

The Spanish theologians evidently think that they are making a concession by allowing us to hold this difference of mode of being, one for the natural Christ, the other for the Eucharistic

* Salmant., tome xviii, p. 304.

Christ. Yet they are persuaded that such a difference is essential to the true understanding of the Eucharistic change. This duality in the mode of being, the natural mode and the sacramental mode, belongs to the heart of the mystery. We are really coming back here to the guiding thought of this whole book, the sacramental state. For more than one believer, without being conscious of it, the Eucharistic Presence is nothing else than a natural presence under a thin disguise. Such, of course, is not the Catholic dogma. Sacraments, as has been said before, are a sphere of reality which has nothing in common with the natural plane of reality. Could Christ be present in his natural reality both in heaven and on earth?—I speak now of his human presence—S Thomas would say that it is not possible. But why make the supposition? We are not treating of natural presences, but of sacramental presences, and the new substantial mode of being, spoken of by the theologians of Salamanca, is nothing else than the sacramental state, as opposed to the natural state of being. Here, again, perfect identity becomes possible through the very dissimilarity of the two states. All our troubles come from an indiscriminate use of ideas, in constantly making notions which belong to the natural state of being do service for sacramental notions.

Another great commentator on S Thomas, Cardinal Cajetan, gives the theologian of the Eucharist this advice, not to proceed on absolute lines of thought, as he would do in the natural order of reality; but " with a light touch " to discourse on the lines of the power of the sacraments and their order: " Suavi tractatu discurrere secundum potentiam sacramentorum eorumque ordinem."*

In connection with the foregoing, we may add a consideration which will stand us in good stead when we come to the practical and daily intercourse with the divine Eucharist. S Thomas admits as a general principle that Christ's humanity, considered in its natural order, is something more important than the sacraments of his humanity: " Ipsa humanitas potior est quam sacramenta humanitatis."† This, of course, applies directly to the Eucharist, for it is in connection with the Eucharist that S Thomas enunciates the axiom. It is difficult to render the adjective *potior;* it means something holding a higher place, being of greater importance, though it need not be superior in

* Cajet., Q. lxxv, Art. i, Com. xi.
† III, Q. lxxx, Art. v.

nature. The occasion for S Thomas to say this is the necessity in which he finds himself to assign the rank, in the gradation of sin, for bad communions. To sin against Christ's divinity is the greatest sin; next comes the sin against Christ's humanity in himself; then the sin committed against the sacrament of Christ's humanity; and, finally, the sin against the ordinary creature. Sin committed against the sacrament of Christ's humanity, were it even a bad communion, is not so great as the sin committed by those who crucified Christ in his own nature. " The sin of those who killed Christ was much greater. Firstly, because that sin was against Christ's body in its proper nature, but this sin is against Christ's body under the sacramental kind. Secondly, because that sin came from an intention of hurting Christ, but not this sin."*

Catholic theology would certainly lose much if at any time the relative position of the natural Christ and the Eucharistic Christ were habitually ignored.

* III, Q. lxxx, Art. v ad 1m

CHAPTER XIX

CONCOMITANCE

MORE than once in the course of this book have I felt it incumbent on me to promise the reader a special chapter on the doctrine of Eucharistic concomitance. I have been conscious all along that, in order to make clear the sacramental character of the Eucharistic sacrifice, I have been keeping back lights and splendours of which my Catholic reader has been aware instinctively. Those high things, the Body and Blood of Christ in the Eucharist, are not isolated; the whole Catholic upbringing of my reader assures him of that. Now the doctrine of concomitance fully justifies those anticipations and instincts of the Catholic mind.

The word " concomitance " is often used by S Thomas. It has been given dogmatic value of the first rank by the Council of Trent. Though it has a very technical sound, it is in reality a most gracious word. Its Latin roots signify, with a redundance of adverb and verb, the act of walking along with someone as a companion—*concomitari*—the roots of which are *cum* (with) and *comes* (companion). The theological meaning in the Eucharistic doctrine of concomitance is this, that the Eucharistic Body and the Eucharistic Blood of Christ are accompanied; they are not alone, they come, as it were, escorted by friends. Those holy things, Body and Blood, are like the centre of a group; they are surrounded by other holy things, without which they do not exist.

But let us be less figurative in speech. Sacramental signification has a definite meaning and a definite result. In all the sacraments, except one, the sacramental signification and the sacramental result cover each other perfectly, so that there is nothing else except the direct sacramental thing. The case is different with the Eucharist. The Eucharist is the sacrament of the Body and the Blood of Christ, of nothing more and nothing less. But as the Body and the Blood of Christ are not found isolated now, and in fact were not isolated at the Last Supper —the only time of their isolation being on Calvary, after Christ's death—the sacrament of the Eucharist has a concomitance, a cortège of splendours. The Body and Blood of Christ on the Christian altar are perfectly identical with the Body and Blood of Christ in heaven; therefore they are on the altar surrounded by all that surrounds them in the Person of Christ in heaven. But let us be very clear about this: this cortège of new splendours has nothing to do with the sacrament, as such. The sacrament can be without them, strictly speaking. The sacrament is only that which it signifies, and the signification is only of the Body and the Blood.

Three expressions meet the student of this part of theology at every turn, in S Thomas, and, as a matter of fact, in all theological works: *vi sacramenti, vi verborum, vi conversionis—* which mean, respectively, in virtue of the sacrament, in virtue of the words of consecration, and in virtue of change or transubstantiation. Whatever is in the Eucharist as the result of one of these three is sacrament. Whatever else may happen to be in the consecrated bread and wine is there *vi concomitantiae.* For a thing to be in the Eucharist in virtue of the sacrament is a profound concept; in fact, it is the all-dominating idea in this divine matter. It is the whole theory of the relationship of signification. God himself, according to S Thomas, in a passage already quoted, deals sacramentally, not naturally, when, he operates in the Eucharist. By *vi sacramenti* is meant that special order of realities which we have so often described.

CONCOMITANCE

In virtue of the words we have in the Eucharist all those things, and only those things, which are contained in the formulas of consecration. Let us take those sacred phrases; let us give literal meaning to every word of them, and we have the enunciation of what there is on the altar. To add a single word would be a blasphemous interference. The sacrament is everything which is expressed by those holy and terse utterances, the consecration words.

In virtue of change we have this, that bread is transubstantiated into Christ's Body and that wine is transubstantiated into Christ's Blood, nothing more. By *vi conversionis* less is represented than by *vi verborum*, because the words of consecration may mean something more than body and blood. The change is the most limited thing in the Eucharistic *processus;* it affects nothing except the material thing in a very definite way. I say this because it is a debated point whether Christ's Hypostatic union is in the Eucharist *vi verborum* or *vi concomitantiae;* it can certainly not be there *vi conversionis;* but it might be there *vi verborum;* for the consecration words might be so construed as not to be intelligible of a body or a blood not hypostatically united. Some theologians think that the possessive pronouns, *meum* and *meus*, in the consecration words, imply Hypostatic union, as no Body or no Blood belonging to Christ is not hypostatically united. The Council of Trent seems to favour this, as we shall see presently. My object here is to show that there ought to be a difference in the meaning attached to *vi verborum* and *vi conversionis*.

It is evident that the latter two expressions of *vi verborum* and *vi conversionis* are contained under the more comprehensive expression *vi sacramenti*, which is truly an all-embracing term directly opposed to that other term, *vi concomitantiae*. I ought to say that S Thomas generally adds an adjective, and speaks of *vi realis concomitantiae*, in virtue of a real concomitance, no doubt with a view to exclude a merely figurative or a merely moral association of realities.

In order to make it clear what is in the Eucharist *vi sacramenti*, Catholic theologians have reduced the Eucharistic realities to a kind of minimum, convinced as they are that in these sublime matters man has no right to go one single step beyond the meaning of God. They all exclude Christ's human Soul from the strictly sacramental content of the Eucharist. Not only are bread and wine not changed into Christ's

Soul, but the Eucharist is something so immediately connected with Body and Blood that the very emphasis of this bodily aspect of the Eucharist excludes the Soul. Bread and wine are changed into Christ's Body and Blood in a truly limited manner, with just enough degree of being to make the words true, and nothing more. " The form, then, of bread is changed into the form of Christ's Body as far as ' form ' gives bodily existence, but not as far as ' form ' gives to the Body to be animated by such or such a soul " (" Convertitur igitur forma panis in formam corporis Christi, secundum quod dat esse corporeum, non autem secundum quod dat esse animatum tali anima ").* By " form " here S Thomas means the scholastic substantial form, and anyone who knows anything about the theory of matter and form will see readily how S Thomas in this passage reduces the result of Transubstantiation to the lowest minimum, compatible with the meaning of the consecration words. It is not my intention to enter into all the philosophic considerations raised by this attitude of Catholic theologians; but it is a supremely precious tradition in the Catholic school of the older type not to speak there, where God has not

* III, Q. lxxv, Art. vi ad 2m.

211

spoken. Moreover, it is through that distinction between the virtue of the sacrament and concomitance that we are able to preserve the sacrificial aspect of the Eucharist.

There is another most enlightening passage of S Thomas which I cannot refrain from quoting, in which he emphasises once more that complete detachment of the Eucharist, considered in its sacramental aspect, from everything that is not Christ's Body and Christ's Blood, visualised in their most simple state of reality. In the third Article of the eighty-first Question S Thomas treats of the communion of the Last Supper when Christ gave to his disciples his Body to eat and his Blood to drink, nay, when he himself partook of them. The query is whether on that occasion the Body was an impassible, a glorious Body. Christ, at that moment, viewed in his natural state, was not in glory. One objector makes this quaint difficulty: " The words of the sacrament are not now of greater power when they are pronounced by the priest in the person of Christ, than when they were pronounced by Christ himself. But now, through the power of the sacramental words, Christ's impassible and immortal body is consecrated on the altar. Therefore it was so then, much more truly."

The answer of S Thomas comprises in a few words the whole difference between the power of the sacrament and concomitance. " The accidents of the body of Christ are in the sacrament through real concomitance, not through the power of the sacrament: through this there is present (only) the substance of the body of Christ; and, therefore, the power of the sacramental words goes as far as to be the cause that under the sacrament there is the body of Christ, whatever may be the accidents that are found in it in reality " (" Accidentia corporis Christi sunt in sacramento ex reali concomitantia, non autem ex vi sacramenti, ex qua est ibi substantia corporis Christi; et ideo virtus verborum sacramentalium ad hoc se extendit, ut sit sub sacramento corpus Christi, scilicet quibuscumque accidentibus realiter in eo existentibus ").*
The phrase " scilicet quibuscumque accidentibus realiter in eo existentibus " is a real stroke of genius. By those accidents of the Body of Christ S Thomas here means his various states, as mortality and glory; they do not enter directly into the nature of the sacrament as such; the sacrament transcends them; the sacrament is equally true, equally potent, equally direct whether Christ be here on earth, as he was at

* III, Q. lxxxi, Art. iii ad 3m.

the Last Supper; whether he be dead on the
cross; whether he dwell with his disciples on
the shores of the lake after the Resurrection;
whether he be ascended to the right hand of
the Father in glory. There is no more reason
why the Eucharist should have vicissitudes and
alterations owing to Christ's wonderful career
in his natural state, than, for instance, the
sacrament of Baptism should be modified in its
innermost constitution according as Christ is
either in heaven or on earth. We do not say,
let it be understood, that Christ's natural states
are not reflected in the Eucharist; have we not
already made it clear with S Thomas that the
Eucharistic Christ would suffer death if the
natural Christ were at any time suffering death ?
The all-important difference is this, that such
mirroring of the Christ-phases of the natural
order in the Eucharist have nothing to do with
the sacrament as such; and, above all, they are
to be excluded from the Eucharist in its sacrificial aspect. As will be seen presently, through
real concomitance, neither the Body is without
the Blood, nor is the Blood without the Body;
but this association is only through real concomitance; it does not interfere with the directness and exclusiveness of the sacramental change
of bread into Flesh, and of wine into Blood,

in which two there is the whole sacramental representation. "Although the whole Christ be under both kinds (through concomitance), it is not in vain (that the sacrament is of both kinds), for, firstly, this is necessary in order to represent Christ's passion in which the blood was apart, separate from the body, and, therefore, in the form of the consecration words of the blood, mention is made of this being poured out."*

Through concomitance, then, the whole glorious Christ is in the Eucharist. This is Catholic faith. S Thomas never doubts it for a moment. "It is absolutely necessary to confess according to Catholic faith that the whole Christ is in this sacrament. We must know, however, that something of Christ is in this sacrament in either of the following ways. In one way through the power of the sacrament; in another way through the natural concomitance. Through the power of the sacrament, then, there is, under the appearances of the sacrament, that into which the pre-existing substance of bread and wine is changed directly, as is signified through the words of the form of consecration, which are the efficient cause in this sacrament, as in all other changes; as when

* III, Q. lxxvi, Art. ii ad 1m.

215

it is said ' this is my body ' or ' this is my blood.' But through natural concomitance all that is found in the sacrament which is joined to that Thing into which the aforesaid change terminates. For if two things are joined together in reality, wherever one is really, the other also must be; it is only through an act of the mind that we distinguish those things which are united in reality."*

The Council of Trent speaks again in Thomistic language and makes supremely clear the difference between sacramental power and concomitance. It calls this latter a " natural connection and concomitance through which the parts of the Lord Christ, who is risen already from the dead, who dies no more, are linked up between themselves." As for Christ's divinity the Council seems to adopt a different phraseology; it says that Christ's divinity is present after the consecration on account " of that admirable hypostatic union with his body and his soul " (" Divinitatem porro propter admirabilem illam ejus cum corpore et anima hypostaticam unionem "). The Council does not range divinity so boldly under concomitance as some theologians have done.

It may be an interesting point for the his-

* III, Q. lxxvi, Art. i.

torian of Catholic dogma to determine the period when it became convincingly clear to the Church in general that the Eucharist contains the whole Person of Christ. Eucharistic phraseology is almost exclusively what we might call sacramental, all through the centuries; it is only recently that it has become prevailingly personal, in the sense of the Eucharist being spoken of as Christ himself. Might we not remark that, in our own days, almost the whole Eucharistic literature, and a vast amount of the Eucharistic worship and devotion, is based more on the concomitant element of the Eucharist than on the sacramental elements of the Eucharist? Nothing could be more legitimate and helpful; we have the whole Christ in the Eucharist; such is Catholic faith. At the same time we ought not to forget the stern exigencies of Catholic dogma; we must remember that the Eucharist is one of the seven sacraments; above all, that the sacrificial aspect of the Eucharist is saved only through our giving due prominence to what is in the Eucharist *vi sacramenti*. Dogmatically, too, this distinction is supremely vital for the defence of the ancient faith. The cult of the Eucharist, independently of Mass and Communion, as it is practised to-day so much, is certainly justified by all we know from the doctrine of concomitance. But even here, let us remember that although the whole Christ is in this sacrament—though not in virtue of this sacrament—he is there *per modum sacramenti*, not in a natural mode of being, but in an entirely new mode of being, the sacramental mode. In other words, even the things of Christ that are in the Eucharist through concomitance, borrow, so to speak, that entirely new mode of existence which S Thomas calls a new *esse*, which makes it imperative on us to speak of the Person of Christ in the Eucharist as being the sacramental Christ.

Theologians have tried their acumen in finding explanations for the presence of the concomitant elements. We know it as a precise dogmatic fact that the Body and Blood of Christ are in the sacrament through Transubstantiation. We do not know, however, how the Soul of Christ is there, as concomitance is not an explanation, like Transubstantiation. S Thomas has refrained from any attempt to go beyond the simple meaning of concomitance. There is certainly in the Eucharist a vast undefined region of mystery, which leaves full scope to the mystic, and of which the Catholic mystic has indeed amply availed himself. We have in the Eucharist the clear island of solid rock, its sacramental aspect, with its sacrificial worth; this is simple and direct in concept, clearly defined by the Councils and by tradition. The island is surrounded by a sea of wonderful mystery, I mean, the vitalities of Christ's infinite Personality.

Some theologians have not been without the courage of their convictions, and have distinguished, in the things belonging to concomitance, between *producibilia et improducibilia* —*i.e.*, things that can be produced and things that cannot be produced.* Divinity itself cannot be produced; the Soul of Christ, to speak of one thing only, can be produced by the power of God as it is a finite thing. The divine things, then, come into the Eucharist in virtue of divine immensity; the finite things, our bold theologians say, are in the Eucharist through an act of God's power similar to that act which changes bread into Flesh and wine into Blood. It is a direct act of God, but in no wise more marvellous than the act which transubstantiates. The Thing which is the Soul of Christ in Heaven, is in the Eucharist through the productive act of God as much as the Flesh and the Blood. And so of the other things that constitute Christ.

* Salmant., tome xviii, p. 64.

There is really no reason why the theologian should not exhibit such boldness of logic. God gives us the Flesh and Blood of Christ as it is in reality; it is immaterial after that whether there be the Soul also, with all the qualities of the Soul, but endowed with a sacramental mode of existence. Only let us bear in mind that Christ's Soul in the Eucharist is not there in virtue of the change, but in virtue of an absolute productive act, which absolute act again, no doubt, is only another aspect of some very simple property of the divine omnipotence.

Once we admit the fundamental principle that God has power to transpose reality and being from one order into the other, from the natural order into the sacramental order, we have committed ourselves to every possible instance of such transposition.

The instance of concomitance more directly concerned with the sacrifice of Mass is this, that now the Body is never without the Blood, and the Blood is never without the Body in the Eucharistic sacrifice. For a good many people this dogmatic fact has obscured the notions of the Eucharistic sacrifice. They seem to be under the impression that, owing to the inseparability of Body and Blood, the Eucharist is not a drastic enough immolation, unless we look elsewhere for sacrificial features. The sacramental Body and Blood do not seem to suffice to their ardour for realities, I might almost say, to their zeal for ethical achievements. This is a strange misreading of the Eucharistic mystery, not to say of the very nature of sacrifice. Do we not give to God in the Eucharistic sacrifice the two things he loves best in this world, the Body and Blood of his Son? That such a Body and such Blood be wrapped up in every kind of glory; that they be even wrapped up in each other, does certainly not interfere with the perfection of the gift, nor with the precise nature of the gift. There would be no sacrifice if the gift were something less than Body and Blood; but why should the presence of fresh glories in the Body and Blood interfere with the sacrifice? Provided we approach God carrying the Flesh and Blood of the Victim, in virtue of our sacramental ministry, we do a clearly-defined sacerdotal thing. That God should make our gift something fuller than does our ministry, how can this create confusion? In these high regions of divine life realities are inseparable; they accompany each other, without destroying each other's individual identity. May we not in this connection think of the Incarnation as a greater instance of sacrament

and concomitance? Out of three divine
Persons, the Second Person only took flesh; yet
we know all along that the Word is not without
the Father and the Holy Ghost, that the three
divine Persons dwell in Christ's humanity.
Yet it is the Son who was born, the Son who
lived and died and rose again, not the Father
nor the Holy Ghost. In divine things abundance of life is the rule; but in this abundance,
division of Persons, divisions of Missions,
remains infinitely clear. In the Eucharist we
have not only an abundance of Christ; we have
the whole Christ. But in the very midst of
that totality the sacrament remains a clear
thing, with a function and a mission all its
own.

CHAPTER XX

MAN'S SHARE IN THE EUCHARISTIC SACRIFICE

AT no turning-point in our theological journey do we see to clearer advantage the sacramental concept of the Eucharistic sacrifice than when we arrive at man's role and share in the great mystery.

The Eucharist is essentially a gift to the Church, not only of Christ, but of the sacrifice of Christ, so that the Church herself has her sacrifice; nay, every Christian has his sacrifice. To participate in Christ's great sacrifice on the cross in a merely utilitarian mode by receiving the benefits of such a sacrifice, is only one-half of the Christian religion. The full Christian religion is this, that the very sacrifice is put into our hands, so that we, too, have a sacrifice, and we act as men have acted at all times when they walked before God in cleanness of faith and simplicity of heart; we offer to God a sacrifice of sweet odour.

There are few sentences in the immense theological output of S Thomas which are such a sign-post at the division of roads as the following phrase from the Third Part of the *Summa*, the sixth Article of the twenty-second Question. It is the portion of the *Summa* where S Thomas treats of Christ's Priesthood: " In nova lege verum Christi sacrificium communicatur fidelibus sub specie panis, et vini " (" In the new law the true sacrifice of Christ is communicated to the faithful under the appearance of bread and wine "). It is evident from the context that S Thomas here speaks not only of the communication of the graces of Christ's sacrifice, but the sacrifice itself, *verum Christi sacrificium*, is communicated and given to them for their possession and use.

The question at issue in that portion of the *Summa* is Christ's Priesthood according to the order of Melchisedech. Is Christ's Priesthood truly according to the order of Melchisedech ? Would it not be better to say that Christ's Priesthood is according to the legal rites of the period that followed the mysterious appearance of Melchisedech, when there were the bloody sacrifices of the Temple, as these came much nearer in character to Christ's sacrifice ? " In the priesthood of Christ," says S Thomas, " we may consider two things, the offering up (*oblatio*) of Christ, and the participation of that offering. As far as the offering up is concerned, the priesthood of the law, with its pouring out of blood, was a clearer figure of this priesthood than is the priesthood of Melchisedech, in which no blood is poured out. But when we come to the participation of the sacrifice and to its effect—and it is there that the excellency of Christ's priesthood above the legal priesthood is more evidently apparent—the priesthood of Melchisedech prefigured it much more expressly, because Melchisedech offered bread and wine, which signify, in the words of S Augustine, the unity of the Church which is constituted by the participation of the sacrifice of Christ."* The Church is one, says S Augustine in so many words, because it has one sacrifice, and that one sacrifice being like the sacrifice of Melchisedech in bread and wine, is truly the sacrifice of Christ handed over bodily to the Church. The Church and her children partake of the fruits of Christ's great sacrifice on the cross, through the offering up of the same sacrifice. Christ's Priesthood, according to the order of Melchisedech, is verified in this, that he has given his Church his own sacrifice under the appearance of bread and wine.

This idea, then, of the *participatio sacrificii*, of making over his own sacrifice to the Church,

* III, Q. xxii, Art. vi ad 2m.

not in results only, but as an act of sacrificial oblation, is our notion of Christ's great gift to his Church. It is thus we must understand all that is said of the Eucharist as being a participation in Christ's sacrifice: it is the sacrifice itself communicated. The highest need of man, if we understand man's needs in their true unchangeable nature—that of offering up to God a perfect thing in sacrifice—finds its satisfaction and realisation in a sacrament, as all its other needs are provided for by some other sacrament. That a sacrament should wash away the dreadful stain of the human race we take readily for granted; that a sacrament should purify our souls from their daily guilt, that a sacrament should strengthen and feed us, all this becomes easily part of our thinking. But let us look higher and think of nobler needs in man's soul. Is there not in us a hunger and thirst for justice; is there not in us the zeal for the glory of God; is there not in us a burning desire to propitiate the divine Majesty for all the sins committed against It? Those cravings, no longer of our passivities but of our activities, shall they not be met by a sacrament of equal rank, of the same plane of spiritual outlook? Our active needs have an active sacrament, the sacrament-sacrifice, which is put at our disposal, to be used by us to our heart's content. Would it not endanger the whole of spiritual life if in spiritual life we were only recipients and nothing else; if the sacramental order were nothing but a divine, unceasing enrichment of man, might it not be in danger of sliding away from God as even heavenly spirits have turned away? But now the centre of the sacramental order is all active, tending towards God, for God's own sake: it is the sacrifice unto God of a most sweet odour.

We have, then, for the daily needs of our intercourse with God a sacrifice worthy of God, the sacrifice offered up by the Son of God himself. The Eucharistic sacrifice is, therefore, essentially the sacrifice of the Church, for the Church's daily use, and by use we mean, above all things, the worship of God. The Eucharistic sacrifice is not, as was the sacrifice on the cross, an offering for the whole world; but being a sacramental thing it is for the Church, for every member of the Church, because it is offered up as the sacrifice of the Church, by the children of the Church. "The result which the passion of Christ brought about in the whole world, this sacrifice brings about in individual man . . . for this reason the Lord also said: (Matt. xxvi) ' This is my blood which will be poured out for you unto the remission of sins.' "*

We cannot give the Eucharistic sacrifice a scope wider than the Church, because it is the Church only that offers it, and she offers it as her own gift. The sacrifice of the cross belongs to the whole world, but the Eucharistic sacrifice belongs to the Church only.

It is of supreme importance in this part of theology to avoid passing beyond the limits of the divine institution. Though the Eucharistic sacrifice contains the thing that made the Calvary sacrifice, it is not a repetition of the universality of the Calvary sacrifice. It may truly be said that without the Church the Eucharistic sacrifice would have no meaning, as it would be a sacrifice without a purpose, the whole object of the Eucharistic sacrifice being this, that the Church should have a clean oblation to offer up to God. If the Eucharistic sacrifice is a power in this world that affects even those who are not in the body of the Church, it is still through the body of the Church that the power is exerted. The Eucharistic sacrifice reaches the infidel, not directly, but through the Church. It cannot be said of the sacrifice of Mass, as it is said of the sacrifice of the cross,

* III, Q. lxxix, Art. i.

that it redeems mankind; but it redeems the soul of the faithful with an abundance of redemption. The sacrifice of Mass is as much a gift to the children of the Church and as exclusive a gift, as, say, the sacrament of penance: but instead of its being a direct cleansing of the soul, it is a direct propitiation and glorification of God.

There is no phrase stamped more clearly on the face of Catholic theology than this, that the Eucharistic sacrifice is offered up always and everywhere *in persona Christi;* Christ must be looked upon as the One who offers the Eucharistic sacrifice as truly as he offered the Calvary sacrifice; this is the Catholic faith. In the great Christian sacrifice the priest and the victim are one and the same. This identity of priest and victim must be preserved at all costs in the Eucharistic sacrifice. Christ is the Priest according to the order of Melchisedech in the sacrifice of bread and wine. As the mortal Christ at the Last Supper offered up for the first time the Eucharistic sacrifice, so does Christ now unceasingly offer up the Eucharistic sacrifice all over the world. Of this we must never lose sight.

How, then, are we to reconcile what we said a moment ago about the Church's privilege of having a sacrifice with that unceasing and insistent exercise of the sacerdotal function by Christ? If the victim and the priest in the Eucharist must be one and the same, how can the Church hope to be the sacrificant herself? Is not this honour entirely appropriated by Christ as much in the Eucharist as it was appropriated by him on the cross? Can the Church hope to do more than to assist at the sacrifice, and to witness it; to stand in awe before it, to veil her face in adoration?

When Christ gave to the Church that sacrifice in which the priest and the victim are always one, he gave her at the same time a priesthood entirely commensurate with the divine offerings, so that the Church should have the joys of the priesthood as well as the benefits of the sacrifice. We have quoted from S Thomas on a former occasion a text which gives in a few words the solution of the apparent difficulty just formulated. The sacrifice which we have from Christ he calls an image of the sacrifice of the cross. The priest of the Church in his sacerdotal capacity is the image of Christ, considered as Priest. In both instances the word has a sacramental meaning of representation: a sacramental priesthood offers up a sacramental sacrifice. There is equation between the sacrifice and the priest; there is the necessary oneness which belongs essentially to the Christian sacrifice. " The celebration of the sacrament is a representative image of Christ's passion. . . . The Altar is representative of the cross itself on which Christ was offered up in his own nature. . . . In the same line of thought also, the priest carries the image of Christ, in whose person and in whose power he pronounces the words in order to consecrate. . . . And thus in a certain way the priest and the victim are the same " (" Et ita quodammodo idem est sacerdos et hostia ").*

This would be the proper place to speak of the nature of the Catholic priesthood. Nothing could be more calculated to bring into a new light the sacramental concept of the Eucharist than a study of that other sacrament, the Christian priesthood. There again we find the sacrament at its best and noblest, doing things in a mode entirely new and *sui generis*. The sacramental character given to the three sacraments of Baptism, Confirmation and Order belongs to that mysterious sphere of things where signs become powers. In virtue of the character of Order the Christian priest bears in himself the image of Christ the Priest, to the

* III, Q. lxxxiii, Art. i ad 2m et 3m.

extent of justifying S Thomas in saying that there is identity in the Eucharist between the priest and the victim. " The sacramental character . . . is a sign bringing about resemblance with one who is the principal in whom there is full authority for that for which someone else is deputed. Thus soldiers who are sent to the battle are sent with the sign of their chief, by which sign they are made like unto him in a way. And thus those who are deputed for the Christian cult, whose author is Christ, receive a character by which they are configured unto Christ. And this is properly the character of Christ."* This character, according to S Thomas again, is in the active powers of the soul, because man is active in his office as priest. For S Thomas sacramental character is the same as *res et sacramentum*. Having, then, a sacramental sacrifice and a sacramental priesthood, the Church is indeed happy in her possessions, and she knows that at no time will her fervour in offering up sacrifices be a derogation of the all-complete sacrifice of Calvary. On the contrary, is it not her very life endlessly to act again, from sheer love, the great role of Christ who is the Priest of God and the Victim of God ? Her priesthood is no more an intrusion

* III, Q. lxiii, Art. iii ad 2m

into Christ's Priesthood than her sacrifice is a supplanting of Christ's sacrifice. In her sacramental genius she knows that her Mass is the living image, the living memory of the holiest thing that ever happened here on earth, the sacrifice of perfect sweetness on Calvary.

Here I make the promise, soon to be fulfilled, that I shall not end this book without saying something of the Christ in glory in his relationship with the daily sacrifice here on earth.

The Church considers that every Mass is a new and a complete sacrifice, because at every Mass a priest acts anew, and does what he did not do the day before. The Eucharistic sacrifice is not one continuous act performed by Christ in heaven; it is so many different sacrifices, with a human mode of differentiation. " In many Masses the offering of the sacrifice is multiplied and, therefore, also the effect of the sacrifice of the Mass " (" In pluribus vero missis multiplicatur sacrificii oblatio: et ideo multiplicatur effectus sacrificii, et sacramenti ").* We must, then, conclude that in the Eucharist Christ is not only the Victim in a sacramental way, but he is also Priest in a sacramental way, not in a natural way as he was Priest in a natural way on Calvary. He is Priest as far as he is

* III, Q. lxxix, Art. vii ad 3m.

represented through the character of Order in the human priest, and as far as he acts through the human priest; in other words, if there were no sacramental priesthood in the Church there could be no sacramental sacrifice. If Christ such as he is now, in his natural state in glory, were directly the sacrificant, there would not be a correspondence between the priest and the victim, as the one would be in the natural state and the other in the sacramental state. But this does not contradict what we said a moment ago that Christ is the High Priest according to the order of Melchisedech, the One who offers up the sacrifice. To offer up the sacrifice through the human priest is essential to a sacramental sacrifice, and it is thus that his great command is carried out, *Hoc facite in meam commemorationem* (" Do this unto a commemoration of me "). What he did at the Last Supper the priests do for ever, in his Name, in his power, in his Person, as the Council of Trent says: they do what he did. He was the first Priest of the Church, and all other priests are his sacramental images. The priesthood which he exercised at the Last Supper as the Head of the Church goes on in the Church in her own priesthood, which is the sacramental continuation of the priesthood of the Last Supper, as the victim is the sacramental representation of the Calvary sacrifice.

The Catholic Church has a very clear practical working method in this holy thing, her sacrifice. What is the sacrificial worth of each individual Mass offered up ? The Church considers that the sacrificial worth of two Masses is just double the sacrificial worth of one Mass; her whole sacramental jurisprudence is based on that principle. This is in perfect conformity with the deepest laws that govern the whole sacramental system given by Christ. Sacraments are not general, universal things; but they are so many sacred acts, each one with a definite spiritual worth. If we let go of the sacramental concept of the Eucharistic sacrifice, I do not see how we could save the individual merit of each Mass, nor how we could defend the Church's jurisprudence in this high matter. But if each Mass is that combination of the human and divine, when the human act of perfect worship has that mysterious prolongation of the divine immolation, we see how each Mass is a definite event in the history of the world. We are not assisting at one continuous sacrifice, immutably offered up by the Christ in heaven, of which our individual Mass would be merely the transient and local manifestation, but, on the contrary,

Mass is offered entirely according to human division of time, often spasmodically. There is one day in the year when it ceases entirely in whole hemispheres; there are more sacrifices one day than another day. Mass is essentially a sacramental action, performed by a sacramental priesthood, not a thing done in heaven, but here on earth, to be numbered in human numbers. It is not one unchanging state of Christ; it is the ever-ardent love of the Church offering up her Christ to the Father, intermittently, yet with an ever-increasing acceleration of activity. " Hostias et preces Tibi Domine laudis offerimus " ("We offer up victim and songs of praise to thee, O Lord ").

The views expressed in this chapter concerning that perfect communication to the Church by Christ of his sacrifice, of his Priesthood, are very definite Tridentine ideas; I must refer my reader again to the twenty-second Session of the Council, of which there is a translation in a former chapter. The language of the Council is so terse that we may read it over and over again before noticing all its implications and all its allusions to the ancient Thomistic theology. Phrases like the following reveal whole spheres of thought which are truly the ancient Catholicism. The Eucharistic mystery is instituted at

236

the Last Supper " in order that Christ might leave behind for his beloved spouse the Church a visible sacrifice, in keeping with man's nature, by which that bloody sacrifice to be offered up once only on the cross would be repeated " (" Ut dilectae sponsae suae Ecclesiae visibile, sicut hominum natura exigit, relinqueret sacrificium, quo cruentum illud, semel in cruce peragendum, repraesentaretur ").* And again, " Christ instituted the new Pasch, giving himself to be immolated by the Church through the priests under visible signs, in memory of his passage from the world to the Father " (" Novum instituit Pascha, seipsum ab Ecclesia per sacerdotes sub signis visibilibus immolandum in memoriam transitus sui ex hoc mundo ad Patrem ").†

This great provision of a sacrifice and of a priesthood which Christ made for his Church, had, according to the Council, one great object, namely, that his Priesthood should not come to an end through death: " Quia tamen per mortem sacerdotium ejus extinguendum non erat."‡ Christ's Priesthood, then, as well as Christ's sacrifice, is perpetuated directly and fully through the institution of the Catholic priesthood and the Catholic sacrifice. It would

* Trent, Sess. xxii, ch. i.   † *Ibid.*   ‡ *Ibid*

be quite a wrong visualising of Christ's Priesthood to think of him as doing the functions of a priest, specifically, in the full sense of the word, in heaven, at the right hand of the Father. If Christ's life in heaven were truly the exercise of priesthood, it would not have been necessary to fear its extinction at his death on the cross as the Council supposes. To prevent such extinction, again in the meaning of the Council, God gave the sacramental priesthood, with the sacramental sacrifice. Christ's resurrection and Christ's glory are not the continuation of the priesthood, but the sacramental offering and the sacramental priesthood are that continuation on which the Council lays such stress.

The whole sacramental doctrine of S Thomas is nothing if not one and harmonious. If the sacramental character of the priest enables him to be the sacrificant in Christ's Person, sacramental character, again, enables the multitude of the faithful to join in that sacrifice in their own way. The sacramental character of Baptism, first, and then the sacramental character of Confirmation, are, for S Thomas, with the sacramental character of Order, though in a lesser degree, figures and resemblances of Christ's Priesthood; and, therefore, every baptised person is radically fit to communicate in

that great sacrifice, to be a sacrificant—at least, by participation. " The sacramental character is a certain participation of the priesthood of Christ in his faithful, so that as Christ has the full power of spiritual priesthood, his faithful also are made like unto him in this, that they participate in the certain spiritual power with respect to the sacraments, and with respect to those things which belong to the divine cult."*
Through that specific spiritual thing, the sacramental character, the Christian people are enabled to take a most personal and most direct part in the Eucharistic sacrifice. Their contact with that sacrifice is something more than by faith and devotion; it is a sacramental contact, their character of Christians answering to the sacrificial aspect of the Eucharist in a way which makes of the sacrifice of Mass and the Christian assembly at Mass a true royal priesthood, in the words of S Peter. " But you are a chosen generation, a kingly priesthood, a holy nation, a purchased people: that you may declare his virtues, who hath called you out of darkness into his marvellous light."†

It has not been my purpose in this chapter to treat more fully of the fruits of the sacrifice of Mass in favour of the Church, of the celebrant,

* III, Q. lxiii, Art. v.   † i Pet. ii 9.

of the layman; this part of our theology has been very well studied, and it is not my intention to give it more of my space. I have been concerned chiefly with the human setting of the great sacramental sacrifice, keeping it, as it were, on this earth, though it be not of this earth. I have tried to show how it is the Church's sacrifice, and therefore our sacrifice; how it is a perpetuation of Christ's role, both as Priest and Victim. We succeed as priests to the Christ of the Last Supper; we are not, when we come to speak in exact language, the representatives of the Christ in glory when we are at the Altar. The glorious Christ is not represented, in strict theological language, by any sacrament; as such he is the consummation of the sacraments, not the content of the sacraments, in their true sacramental inwardness.

CHAPTER XXI

THE EUCHARISTIC LITURGY

THE eighty-third Question of the Third Part of the *Summa* of S Thomas is all about the rite of the sacrament of the Eucharist. The great Doctor becomes a liturgist. It is remarkable that the very first article in his lengthy analysis of the liturgical setting of the Eucharist is the extremely important query " Whether Christ be immolated in this sacrament ?" a query, as we have already seen, answered by the Doctor in the affirmative. By subsuming the Eucharistic immolation under the Eucharistic rite, S Thomas once more shows clearly how radically sacramentarian is his concept of Mass. The Eucharistic rite is either sacramental signification in its essential aspect, or the extension and the enlargement by the Church, under the guidance of the Holy Ghost, of the sacramental formulas of divine origin. When S Thomas makes Christ's immolation on the altar to be part of the Eucharistic rite, he evidently gives to immolation a more active than passive meaning. From his very context he shows that he considers the Church to be the one who immolates Christ on the Altar by doing the great sacramental deed. S Thomas does not really consider the hidden and mysterious things that happen behind the veil of the Eucharistic appearances, whether Christ be in some unknown form of passive immolation; but to him the Church truly immolates Christ as she performs the great sacrament, because the sacrament is the literal representation of the Calvary immolation. The Church immolates because she consecrates.

The Eucharistic rite, or, if you like, Eucharistic Liturgy, is a fresh confirmation, if fresh confirmation were necessary, of the thesis of this book, that the great Catholic tradition visualises the Eucharistic sacrifice from the angle of sacrament. The Church has surrounded the sacrifice of the Eucharist with such splendour, with such rites and ceremonies as could only adorn a thing entirely in the Church's possession. Sacraments are the property of the Church, if anything is the property of the Church, and, being her own, she has acted with them with the utmost resourcefulness, adding to the divinely instituted significations which constitute the essence of the sacrament her own symbolisms and signs and sacramentals, so as

242

to make of the simple thing given by Christ a glorious celebration, where nature and grace, art and faith, vie with one another in the effort to express the great hidden truth.

It is my contention, then, that such behaviour on the part of the Church is possible only because the Church considers the sacrifice delivered unto her to be a great sacramental function. She has to perform that function, and she does it with a genius truly divine.

Justin, one of the earliest and most authentic authorities on the Eucharistic rite of the primitive Church, already speaks of that fertility of inspiration which evidently surrounded the celebration of the Eucharistic mysteries from the very beginning. The celebrant is said by him to offer up Eucharists with great abundance, as much as his strength allows, clearly pointing to a liberty of improvisation which had not been checked by definite Canons of Liturgy.* The one remarkable fact of the various Liturgies, both of East and West, is this, that sacrificial language and sacrificial rites are used with great liberty and richness, before and after the essential words of consecration, so that it becomes often a puzzle at first sight whether the *oblata*, the things offered, the things sacri-

* *Apol.*, lxv et lxvii.

ficed, are bread and wine or the Body and Blood of Christ; but there is really no puzzle if we remember the profoundly sacramental character of the sacrifice. The Church's act of offering and oblation is inseparable from the divine contents which at a given moment are brought into her *oblata*. Being an institution composed of men, the Church acts like a human being, multiplying words and signs in order to express a truth too great for expression. The Church, in the very midst of the Eucharistic sacrifice, remembers the ancient sacrifices of Abel, Abraham and Melchisedech, and implores God to look upon her sacrifice with as great favour as he looked on those sacrifices. Such humility is quite comprehensible if we remember again the sacramental character of the Church's divine sacrifice. It is true that the thing which she offers is infinitely greater than the offerings of Abel and Abraham and Melchisedech together, but as she is the sacrificant she craves God's favour, as she might be after all unworthy of presenting so holy a sacrifice.

In other words, the sacrifice of Mass is a profoundly human thing, in the sense in which all the sacraments are human things; divine in their innermost kernel, indestructible in their nature, unassailable by man's iniquity, they are still human in their whole active policy; they expand or become narrow, they shine or are obscured, they speak or are silent, as man, who has their life in his hands, is either generous or niggardly, a child of light or a child of darkness, one who is deaf or one who has his ears open to the things of God. Nowhere else in the realm of reality do we find things that are so absolutely finished in themselves, so complete, and so divine as are the sacraments, which, on the other hand, are left so entirely to man's activities for new fertilities and new perfections. This is the whole sacramental mystery, and the Eucharist is the most perfect instance of it.

Eucharistic Liturgy, then, may be considered as an expansion by the Church of the sacramental signification. Suppose the Eucharistic sacrifice to be what some are inclined to make it, an entirely divine act, done by Christ, of which the Church is merely the witness, in which she has no part as sacrificant, as a sacramental power, there could be really no Eucharistic Liturgy, in the true sense of the word. There could be hymns and canticles sung around the altar, as we could sing hymns to commemorate the creation of all things, but we should be merely a circle of worshippers, whilst the Liturgy is essentially an act, a doing of a mystery, an expansion of a central sacred thing. We celebrate Mass, let us remember that; we do not only sing at Mass, we make the divine sacrifice, so simple in its essence, dwell amongst us; we detain it amongst us, we are reluctant to see its end, we love to have our hands on the divine Victim for a long time, till our whole being is thrilled with love and awe. The Church has certainly considered that she has power over the great sacrifice; it being her own possession, she makes it last, she makes it long or short to suit her devotion.

It is sometimes asked, When does Mass really begin—I mean the essential and technical moment of the sacrifice? When does it end? The true answer to this ought to be simply that Mass ends when the Church ceases voluntarily to be considered as a sacrificant. No one word or act of Mass can be pointed out as containing the whole essence of the sacrifice. The thing which Christ did at the Last Supper was not so simple as might appear at first sight. It must have been, on the whole, a prolonged rite, intermingled with the Jewish Pasch, yet easily discernible from it. The Christian Mass, likewise, has never been so simple as certain admirers of primitive forms would like us to believe. Consecration of bread and wine, followed sooner or later by the partaking of the consecrated elements, are essential to Mass; but it would be difficult, not to say impossible, to give intrinsic reasons why the sacrifice is said to be finished, if we had not the very clear rite of the Church, with a beginning and an ending, like all other sacraments. If consecrated wine were preserved in the Tabernacle as consecrated bread is preserved, this would not mean the continuation of the sacrifice of Mass, as the Church would no longer be the actual sacrificant.

When our Lord told his Apostles to do this in memory of him, he evidently ordered them to carry out the rite which they had seen him perform, with its thanksgiving, its blessing, its breaking of the divine elements, and other wonderful circumstances, which must have made such a deep impression on their minds.

The institution of this great sacrament is different from the institutions of the other sacraments narrated in the Gospels; the Apostles are commanded directly to baptise all nations, they are given power to remit all sins in general terms, without any restrictions. The case is different with the Eucharist; they are told to do what they had seen with their own eyes. They are not told to consecrate bread and wine, much less are they told to change bread into the Body of Christ or wine into his Blood. The command is of a much sweeter nature: " Hoc facite in meam commemorationem." The *hoc* means all that they had seen and witnessed in the Upper Room. In no other sacrament is rite or liturgy such a constituent element of the sacramen titself: *Et antiquum documentum novo cedat ritui* (" Let the old form give way before the new rite ").

The sacrifice of Mass, then, being in its very nature a sacramental rite, has always possessed in the history of the Catholic Church more the appearance of a feast than of a sad memory; we do not make of our daily Mass a Good Friday Liturgy, in which Christ's agony on the cross is so visibly brought to our imagination. On the contrary, Mass is all rejoicing; it is the feast of the Church; it is surrounded by every possible splendour; its character—or shall we say, its æsthetic side?—is borrowed, not from Calvary, but from the spacious Upper Room of the Last Supper, where the Son of God was surely a splendid Host. The great sacrifice of the Eucharist does not come to us out of an invisible world with the rapidity and the power of lightning; it is not an act of God in the sense in which the creation of light was an act of God;

it is human beyond words; it is the feast of love; it is the sacrament of union; it is the banquet which Christ with a great desire wished to eat with his disciples. From the repast of the Supper room the transition into the sacrificial act of the Eucharist was almost insensible. The humanity of it all is simply overpowering, and if it is true that *sacramenta sunt propter homines*, is it not also true that *sacramenta sunt sicut homines?* Sacraments are deeply human. And is there anything more human in the history of the human heart than the celebration of the first Mass when John, the well-beloved, was resting his head on the breast of the divine High Priest?

CHAPTER XXII

THE EUCHARISTIC BANQUET

WE have come nearly to the end of our book, and perhaps more than one reader may be mildly shocked to find that a book could be written on the Eucharist with so little about Holy Communion. But let me assure my patient friend who has followed me so far that nothing is dearer to me than the Bread of Life. I could write him a whole book on the subject, and not say all I would love to say. But as this little effort bears the name of *A Key to the Doctrine of the Eucharist*, I am not so much a dispenser of the divine Bread as an opener of the mystical Bethlehem, the House of Bread. The Bread of Life, the Eucharist as the food of man, is not to be found anywhere and everywhere, but it is essentially a thing from the altar. " The chalice of benediction which we bless, is it not the communion of the blood of Christ ? And the bread which we break, is it not the partaking of the body of the Lord ? . . . Behold Israel according to the flesh. Are not they that eat of the sacrifice partakers of the altar?"* At no time ought we to surrender this great Christian privilege that we are partakers of the altar of God. It is the glory of the Eucharistic bread that it is not ordinary divine bread, but a bread from the altar of God.

There ought not to be in classical Christianity a real division of spiritual attitude between Mass and Communion. Suppose, *per impossibile*, that there were an extreme multiplicity of private communions by the faithful, on the one hand, and an ever-dwindling attendance at the sacrifice of Mass on the other hand, it would indeed be the gravest spiritual disorder; it would falsify the Eucharistic setting; it would lower the sacrament through a misconception of its true role. The *usus sacramenti*, as S Thomas calls it constantly, the use of the sacrament, follows upon the sacrament according to that terse phrase on which we have already commented. The sacrament-sacrifice is followed by the sacrament-food. Such was the order at the institution of the Eucharist, when Christ himself partook, before giving to his Apostles, thus completing in his own Person the whole Eucharistic sacrament.

It is anything but service done to this greatest

* 1 Cor. x 16, 18.

of the Catholic sacraments to describe Holy Communion in terms which many a pantheist might love. The union with God when we eat the Bread of Life takes hold of us in a very definite portion of our spiritual being; it brings us back, as all sacraments do bring us back, to the passion of Christ; we take and eat the holy Thing that is offered up, the Body; we drink the cup of the testament in the Blood of Christ. Communion is a sacramental thing, and in this it differs from those other visitations of the spirit which lead men to God, not sacramentally but personally.

Divine things are wonderfully ordered; they do not encroach on each other, their functions are not interchangeable. Not all the spiritual work is done by the sacrament; the Spirit himself bloweth where he listeth; Eucharistic Communion is not all communion with God; but it is a definite communion with the Christ who shed his Blood for us.

The sixth chapter of the Gospel of S John, where Christ announces the gift of the Bread of Life, is no mere promise of a new manna coming down from heaven without passing through the altar of sacrifice. " The bread of God is that which cometh down from heaven and giveth life to the world."* Now that

* John vi 33.

Bread of God, Christ himself, comes down from heaven, not merely as a thing falling gently to the ground, just to be gathered up by man, but it comes down from heaven with the set purpose of a sacrificial nature: "Because I came down from heaven not to do my own will, but the will of him that sent me."* If he is the living Bread, a Bread that will give life to the world, it is because he first has given his Flesh for the life of the world. " This is the bread which cometh down from heaven: that if any man eat of it, he may not die. I am the living bread which came down from heaven. If any man eat of this bread he shall live for ever: and the bread that I will give is my flesh, for the life of the world."† These last words, " And the bread I will give is my flesh, for the life of the world," have a clear sacrificial ring about them. Moreover, that emphatic distinction between flesh and blood, which is such a marked feature of Christ's discourse at Capharnaum, is clearly an allusion to the ever-recurring sacrifices of flesh and blood.

The Eucharistic banquet, then, is essentially a sacrificial banquet: as such it makes an impassable gulf between light and darkness, between the world and God, between Satan and

* John vi. 38.　　　　　† John vi. 50-52.

Christ. " You cannot drink the chalice of the Lord and the chalice of devils: you cannot be partakers of the table of the Lord and the table of the devils."* The chalice of the devils and the table of the devils in this text are not metaphorical, immaterial things as might appear to some who are always eager to give to the Eucharistic texts of the Scriptures merely symbolical meaning. St Paul means a very material thing, the meats that come from the altar before the idol in the heathen temples. " But the things which the heathens sacrifice, they sacrifice to devils and not to God. And I would not that you should be made partakers with devils."†

Do any of my readers still remember the ancient theological distinction between the " sacrament," the " sacrament and thing," and the " thing " which I have explained in a former chapter ? It is a favourite idea with S Thomas that the " thing " of the sacrament, or, if you like, the sacramental grace, is the mystical Body of Christ; Christ's sacramental Body makes Christ's mystical Body. The whole Eucharistic spirit is a spirit of charity, a spirit between the members of Christ. Here again S Paul says the trenchant word: "For we, being many, are one bread, one body: all that partake of one

* 1 Cor. x 21.   † *Ibid.*, v 20.

bread."* The sacrament signifies this society of the elect, as it signifies the true Body of Christ. So much is S Thomas convinced of this membership with Christ's mystical Body being the essence of the Eucharistic grace in the soul of man that he sees there the reason why communion in mortal sin is not only a grievous offence, but is actually a sacrilege. " Whosoever, then, receives the sacrament, signifies by that very fact that he is united to Christ and incorporated into his members. Now this (union with Christ) takes place through faith fully informed (with charity) which no one can possess with the guilt of mortal sin. And therefore it is manifest that whosoever receives the sacrament with the guilt of mortal sin on him, commits a falsehood against this sacrament, and accordingly he incurs a sacrilege as one who violates the sacrament; and for this reason he sins mortally."†

Membership with Christ and the whole mystical Body of Christ ought to be considered to be the specific Eucharistic grace, as distinguished from all other graces. " Qui manducat meam carnem et bibit meum sanguinem, in me manet, et ego in illo. Sicut misit me vivens Pater, et ego vivo propter Patrem: et qui mandu-

* 1 Cor. x 17.   † III, Q. lxxx, Art. iv.

cat me, et ipse vivet propter me."* To make this profession of divine membership in a state of mortal sin is a direct violation of the truth of things. S Thomas reasons out that heinous offence to its logical consequences; he calls it in the text quoted: " *Falsitatem in hoc sacramento,*" a falseness in the very midst of the sacrament.

The Eucharistic sacrifice is profoundly a corporate act; it is the act of the Church herself; we are never isolated worshippers in the great rite, even when we are but a few gathered at the altar in some remote church, as we are in communion with the whole Catholic Church. But the eating of the divine offering is again invested with social significance. We become all members of one Body, eating one Bread: this is the classical, traditional concept of the Eucharistic assemblies of Christians. The society of the elect here on earth are gathered in love and brotherhood, performing such mysterious rites as will open the portals of heaven itself, and make Angels and men come together. It would be a disastrous day for the Christian cause if, in the minds of the faithful, the Eucharistic mystery were shorn of that all-important social character, if their frequent eating of the

* 1 John vi 57, 58.

heavenly Bread meant to them nothing but individual spiritual satisfaction, without furthering the great cause of Christ's mystical Body, the society of the elect.

The world's salvation is in the Eucharist. This is not a hyperbolical phrase; it is a sober statement of spiritual reality. The world's salvation is its approximation to the redemptive mystery of Christ. If this mystery becomes the constant occupation of human society, its daily deed, its chief concern, its highest aspiration, then society is saved. Holy Mass is the difference between paganism and Christianity, let us be under no illusion. There is no charity possible as an institution, as a thing that is a world-power, outside the sacrament of Christ's mystical Body. The ideal world of which the saint dreams is a human society where there is practical knowledge of the meaning of the Eucharistic sacrifice, where men and women have a clear comprehension of the divine mysteries, and where purity and justice are cherished because without them men would be unfit for the Communion of the Body of God.

CHAPTER XXIII

EUCHARISTIC CONSUMMATION

WE have seen in one of the earlier chapters that every sacrament has an intimate connection with the future life: "*Et futurae gloriae nobis pignus datur.*" Sacraments are true prophecies of the eternal glories. S Thomas calls the sacrament "*prognosticum futurae gloriae.*"* The sacramental graces, taken in their most specific aspect, have this characteristic of being a pledge of the eternal splendours of the life to come. " In whom (Christ) also believing, you were signed with the Holy Spirit of promise, who is the pledge of our inheritance, unto the redemption of acquisition, unto the praise of his glory."† Not only do we receive graces through the sacraments which give us strength to fight the battle of our soul and to conquer eternal life, but in them we are marked and sealed for eternal life. " He that eateth my flesh and drinketh my blood hath everlasting life; and I will raise him up in the last day."‡

* III, Q. lx, Art. iii.　† Eph. i 13, 14.　‡ John vi 55.

There is, however, in the Catholic sacramental system a character of transitoriness which it is very important to remember. S Thomas never tires of alluding to the instrumental worth of the sacraments. They are the tools of God to bring about definite results, and when those are completely achieved the tool will be laid aside by the divine Artificer. Sacraments are part of the work which Christ does here on earth; they are not permanent glories of the everlasting triumph, " when God shall be all in all." They belong to that definite *opus* which Christ achieved here below, a task very clearly set him by the Father, to be done in its own hour. " I have glorified thee on the earth; I have finished the work which thou gavest me to do."*

The greatest of the sacraments, the Eucharist, is no exception to this law of transitoriness. The Eucharist, divine as it is, will pass away as faith and hope will pass away; but the graces of the sacrament, the *res sacramenti*, will remain for all eternity, in the perfection of Christ's Mystical Body. The glory for which the Eucharistic mystery prepares us is something greater than the Eucharistic mystery itself. This is admitted by S Thomas in the second Article of the seventy-ninth Question.

* John xvii 4.

259

An objector says: "What is greater cannot be brought about by what is smaller, because nothing acts beyond the limits of its own kind; but it is a smaller thing to receive Christ under a foreign kind, *sub specie aliena*, as happens in the sacrament, than to possess him in the proper kind, *in specie propria*, a thing that belongs to glory; therefore the sacrament does not cause the acquisition of glory." In the answer S Thomas emphasises the instrumental character of the Eucharist: " To the third difficulty I say that it is the very nature of a sacrament that Christ should be taken under a foreign kind, as a sacrament acts instrumentally, for nothing prevents an instrumental cause from producing an effect which is greater than itself."

Divine as the Eucharist is, life with Christ in heaven will be something diviner still. There will be truly no spiritual waste; when the long day of God's work on the souls of men will be ended, God will be found to have given the Bread of Life, the flesh of his Son, with lavish liberality to those who were doing the work of God; but as the work of God was this, to come to Christ in his glory, and as countless multitudes will have come to Christ in his glory, the heavenly Father will be found to have been a generous householder, but not a wasteful one.

The Eucharistic sacrifice shares in the transitoriness of the whole sacramental system; its sacramental character postulates this. There will be no Eucharistic sacrifice in heaven, as there will be no Baptism, as there will be no anointing with chrism. The Lamb of God will be wedded to his Bride, the Church, and the sacrifice of the Lamb will be succeeded by the nuptials of the Lamb.

It has been a tendency of pious minds to give to the Eucharistic mystery, and above all, to the Eucharistic sacrifice, a heavenly prolongation, not in the sense of all things reaching consummation through the power of the Eucharist, but in the sense of a real continuation of the Eucharistic immolation in its proper kind. Some have spoken of the *sacrificium coeleste* as being the third member of a great sacrificial plan of which the two first members would be the Calvary sacrifice and the earthly Eucharistic sacrifice. This introduces a useless confusion into theological thought. Heaven has no sacrifice, but is the consummation of all sacrifices. Sacrifice belongs to the period of faith and hope, where things are seen in a dark manner. To introduce sacrificial elements into the clarity of divine vision is to give to the notion of sacrifice an arbitrary extension. In heaven sacrifices are ratified, are received, are remembered, but they are not celebrated; heaven sings the glory of the sacrifice as the triumph of the past, as one remembers the day of battle of long ago on which a nation was born to liberty: " And they sung a new canticle, saying: Thou art worthy, O Lord, to take the book and to open the seals thereof: because thou wast slain and hast redeemed us to God, in thy blood, out of every tribe and tongue and people and nation: and hast made us to our God a kingdom and priests. And we shall reign on the earth."* Whatever we read in the Scriptures of the glories of the Lamb has reference to the great day when the Lamb was slain on this earth.

It is clear that S Thomas knows of no *sacrificium coeleste* in the true sense of a sacrifice. All sacrificial activity is in the militant Church. The heavenly Christ is for S Thomas even now, whilst on earth there is the daily sacrifice, in a state of consummation, not in a state of immolation. Now immolation and consummation are contradictory terms in theology; they cannot be predicated of the same person at the same time, under the same aspect. The Eucharistic Christ is immolated; the natural Christ in heaven is consummated; these are two

* Apoc. v 9, 10.

different aspects of the same Christ; but the heavenly Christ is not at the same time consummated and immolated. Christ's Priesthood is eternal, not because the sacrifice is everlasting, but because the consummation of the sacrifice is eternal. This is the doctrine of S Thomas. "Does Christ's priesthood remain for all eternity?" is the title of the fifth Article of the twenty-second Question in Part Three of the *Summa*. How could Christ's Priesthood be eternal, as priesthood is necessary to those only who have the infirmity of sin which may be expiated by the sacrifice of the priest? But among the saints in heaven there will be no infirmity of sin. "My answer is, that in the office of a priest two things are to be considered, firstly the very offering of the sacrifice, and secondly, the consummation of the sacrifice, which latter is to be found in this, that the end of the sacrifice is reached by those for whom the sacrifice is offered. Now the ends of the sacrifice which Christ offered up were not temporal goods, but eternal goods, to which we reach through his death; so it is said in Heb. ix that Christ is ' come an high priest of the good things to come.' For this reason Christ's priesthood is said to be eternal. This consummation of Christ's sacrifice was prefigured by the high priest of the law entering once a year into the holy of holies with the blood of the goat and calf, as it is said in Lev. xvi; whilst, on the other hand, he did not immolate the goat and the calf in the holy of holies, but had immolated them outside; as in like manner Christ entered unto the holy of holies, that is to say, into heaven itself, and prepared unto us the way of entering in there through his blood, which he poured out for us on this earth."*

It is clear from this that S Thomas, with his firm belief in the eternal Priesthood of Christ, admits of no immolation in heaven. Heaven only knows consummation.

A few more phrases from the same Article will be edifying. " The Saints who will be in heaven will not be in need any longer of purification through Christ's priesthood; but having been purified, they will be in need of consummation through that same Christ on whom their glory depends. It is said, therefore, in the twenty-first chapter of the Apocalypse, that the glory of God enlightens it, namely, the city of the saints, and that the Lamb is the lamp thereof." . . .† " Although the passion and the death of Christ are not to be renewed any more, the power, however, of that victim once offered,

* III, Q. xxii, Art. v.   † *Ibid.*, ad 1m.

264

abides for ever, as it is said in the tenth chapter to the Hebrews, that by one oblation he has consummated for ever them that are sanctified."*

Eternity of priesthood in Christ, in the mind of S Thomas, is a very definite thing. That glory which was purchased for the elect through the great sacrifice here on earth, natural and sacramental, still depends on the Lamb, who is truly the illuminator of all those who see the Face of God. Christ will show unto the elect that Father whose Countenance shines in infinite graciousness because the sweet odour of the ancient sacrifice remains eternally in the remembrance of God.

The altar which figures so prominently in the Apocalypse is not the altar of the holocaust, but the altar of incense. In Exodus the children of Israel receive God's order to fashion articles for the divine worship. The altar of incense and the altar of holocaust are different in style and purpose: "And all the multitude of the children of Israel being gathered together, he said to them: These are the things which the Lord hath commanded to be done. . . . The altar of incense and the bars and the oil of unction and the incense of spices: the hanging at the door of the tabernacle: The altar of holocaust, and its

III, Q. xxii, Art. v ad 2m.

grate of brass, with the bars and vessels thereof: the laver and its foot."* In S John's vision there is no altar of the holocaust; there only remains the altar of incense. " And another angel came and stood before the altar, having a golden censer: and there was given to him much incense, that he should offer of the prayers of all saints, upon the golden altar which is before the throne of God. And the smoke of the incense of the prayers of the saints ascended up before God from the hand of the angel. And the angel took the censer and filled it with the fire of the altar and cast it on the earth: and there were thunders and voices and lightnings and a great earthquake."†

The offerings laid on that heavenly altar are no longer Body and Blood, but the prayers of the saints. From the Apocalyptic altar there proceed not mercy and forgiveness, but justice and judgement: " Thunders and voices and lightnings and a great earthquake." It is evidently the altar of consummation, not the altar of propitiation.

Prayer there is in heaven—at least, till the great day of the final triumph. Christ in heaven makes unceasing intercession for us. But prayer and sacrifice are not in the same category of

* Exod. xxxv 1, 15, 16.   † Apoc. viii 3, 4, 5.

spiritual realities, though they both belong to the office of a priest. S Thomas teaches that Christ could pray for himself, but that he could not offer up his sacrifice for himself.* Nothing would be less justifiable than to argue from the continuation of Christ's intercession in heaven to the continuation of Christ's immolation in heaven.

It would be equally impossible to find in the Tridentine presentment of the Christian sacrifice any room for the *sacrificium coeleste ;* Trent knows only of the sacrifice accomplished here on earth. The Tridentine Fathers cling to the duality of the bloody sacrifice of Calvary and the unbloody sacrifice of the sacrament; the sacrifice in glory is no part of their theology; in fact, it could not be fitted in with their theology. " If anyone says . . . that Christ has not ordered the Apostles and other priests to offer up his Body and his Blood, let him be anathema."†

A *sacrificium coeleste* could not be Body and Blood, as Christ in heaven is in fulness of his glory. The sacrifice which Christ, according to Trent, ordered the Church to offer is the sacrifice of his Body and his Blood, not the sacrifice of himself in glory. If there were

* III, Q. xxi, Art. iv, and Q. xxii, Art. iv.
† Trent, Sess. xxii, Can. ii.

now a sacrifice truly going on in heaven, our Eucharistic sacrifice here on earth, by the very nature of the supposition, would be merely the earthly representation of that heavenly act. The heavenly act would be continuous, the earthly representations would be successive; but this is not Trent, of course. Body and Blood in the historic sense are the Tridentine notion of sacrifice.

The anathema I have quoted happens to fulfil literally the promise of my Foreword, that we should come back to the point of our departure. We started in the simple faith that at Mass we offer up the Body and the Blood of Christ; and to this simple faith we come back now, well persuaded that it is the whole truth.

But I should not like to leave my reader, who has been so patient with me, with the thunder of an anathema in his ears, though the Church's anger be not against him, but against those evil men who have cast such a blight on the Western mind, when, with their insidious theology, they paralysed it, and rendered it incapable of entering into the glories of Christ's Priesthood here on earth. My conclusion will be an official *protestatio* which Gregory XIII exhorts every priest to recite before he approaches the Altar. It is the truly sober Roman summary of the

Eucharistic attitude of the Catholic mind. " I want to celebrate Mass and to make the Body and the Blood of our Lord Jesus Christ according to the rite of Holy Roman Church, to the honour of Almighty God, and the whole triumphant Court, for my utility and the utility of the whole militant Court, for all those who have commended themselves to my prayers, both in general and in particular, and for the happy state of the Holy Roman Church " (" Ego volo celebrare Missam, et conficere Corpus et sanguinem Domini nostri Jesu Christi, juxta ritum sanctae Romanae Ecclesiae, ad laudem omnipotentis Dei, totiusque Curiae triumphantis, ad utilitatem meam totiusque Curiae militantis, pro omnibus qui se commendaverunt orationibus meis in genere et in specie, et pro felici statu sanctae Romanae Ecclesiae."